Key Buildings of the Twentieth Century

Volume 1 : Houses 1900–1944

David Dunster

The Architectural Press · London

First published in 1985 by The Architectural Press Limited, 9 Queen Anne's Gate, London SW1H 9BY

© David Dunster 1985

British Library Cataloguing in Publication Data
Key buildings of the twentieth century
Vol 1: Houses 1900-1944
1 Architecture, Modern—20th century
I Dunster, David
724.9'1 NA680

ISBN 0-85139-894-4

Printed in Great Britain by Mackays of Chatham

Graphic Design by Annelies Siero

While every reasonable effort has been made to trace copyright owners, it has not always been possible to do so.
On the pages given below, thanks for permission to reproduce photographs are due to those whose names follow the page number.

15 Swedish Architecture Museum (photo Lennart af Petersen).
25, 33, 93 from *Encyclopédie de l'Architecture Nouvelle* by Alberto Sartoris, published by Hoepli, Milano.
41 from *Town and Revolution* by Anatole Kopp, published by Thames and Hudson (photo Konstantin Melnikov, Moscow).
45 from *Wassili u. H. Luckhardt* by Udo Kultermann, published by Verlag Ernst Wasmuth, Tübingen.
51 from *Twentieth Century Houses* by Raymond McGrath, published by Faber and Faber.
102 from *The Work of Oscar Niemeyer,* By Stamo Papadaki, published by Van Nostrand Reinhold Co Inc.
103 from *L'Architecture d'Aujourd'hui.*

This is primarily a book of plans, and the photographs that do appear are intended only to play a supporting role. Even so, the buildings illustrated are in many cases no longer extant, and good photographs of them are often hard to obtain at a price which would keep the book within the range of student readers. It has therefore been necessary in some cases to make use of material which is archival in character, and readers are begged to show understanding of this problem.

CONTENTS

Will the history of modern architecture ever be written? While serious debates continue on both the meaning of modern architecture and the methods of architectural history, no conclusive answer can be offered. Written histories are either polemic or catalogues, narratives or gossip. As an alternative, pictorial histories — such as the Smithsons' and Middleton's 'The Heroic Age of Modern Architecture' — provide an archive of the self-perceptions of the 20s and 30s. 'Key Buildings of the Twentieth Century' Volume 1 is the first drawn history, and it tries to provide evidence for understanding the recent past.

Of all possible modes of representation, the plan — rather than the model — occupies a privileged place in the 20th century. Where Beaux Arts dogmas looked to the plan to demonstrate ideas of movement through hierarchically organized space, Modern Movement architecture looked at plans for descriptions of ways of life. This did invite vast and often crude generalizations on the part of the architect; often the client became an adjunct to the plan, itself an abstraction towards universality. The client is only represented in the abstraction of the plan by specific but small spaces. The house, in its plans, can then only hint at the individual client's personality, which may easily be subsumed by the architect — and particularly by that aspect of his thought which looked forward to a better way of life.

Forty-eight house plans designed between 1900 and 1944 indicate two changes: the first concerns the demands of those who can afford to build new; the second shift records the changes in architectural thinking in this century. The book begins with a country house and ends with a bridge, indicating the architectural shift towards metaphor; while in social terms there is a retreat of private space into the bedroom. And, of course, the live-in servant becomes increasingly rare.

The buildings I selected for the following reasons: first, every major architect is represented — with the exception of Aalto, whose houses are surely his weakest point. Not all the buildings are by any means masterpieces, and some are not typical of an architect's output (for example Mendelsohn and Häring). The conventional historical canon of Modern Movement masters was accepted in compiling the book. Exceptions to this are Lutyens, Hoffmann, and Guimard, all of whom are included by way of contrast. The examples from the 1940s are South American: Oscar Niemeyer and Amancio Williams, both coherently pursued the Modern Movement, at a time when few buildings were constructed in Europe or America. Secondly, there is a range of house sizes, from the largest which is probably Hoffmann's Palais Stoclet, to the smallest which may be Oud's hut. Thirdly, houses were picked because they represented the very many ways in which the problem of the private house has been dealt with by architects.

All the drawings have been completely redrawn from published material. The process of re-drawing was to blow up the published material to a scale of 1:100. The drawings were then all reduced to exactly the same scale, 1:250, which provided the basis for the layout.

Photographs have been added where available, but this is not primarily a photographic book.

All the drawings were re-drawn to a set of conventions, using the same line thicknesses, drawing walls in a thick black line, and drawing tiling patterns for ease of reading. A key to rooms is provided to each house. The texts accompanying each building describe the organization.

If there was a model for this volume, it is F R S Yorke's 'The Modern House', first published in 1934. Yorke was interested in demonstrating that the Modern Movement was an international movement, though he was not as concerned as Hitchcock and Johnson to show that it was an international style. As his writing makes plain, he was very interested in the materials and forms of construction. Many of these materials were proprietary brands available only during the period of construction; and while his book is an invaluable source of this kind of information, without proper constructional sections, much of it is ambiguous – and certainly does not clarify the problems of jointing materials together which led to those difficulties of weathering that gave 'white architecture' a bad name.

Yorke's book, and Raymond McGrath's 'Twentieth Century Houses' of that same year, and magazines of the period, are fascinating sources. In retrospect, there was an avant-garde new architecture for the 20th century which these compilations greeted with enthusiasm. The private house was the functional type which generated most response, simply because it was difficult for young and untried architects who were most excited by the new architecture to receive commissions for large building projects. The history of the League of Nations project provided not only Le Corbusier and Pierre Jeanneret with a bitter experience of the hurdles to be crossed, but also widely publicized these problems of dealing with large commissions. 'The Modern House' therefore acquired early on the status of a bible, not only in England but also in Europe and America.

But as McGrath pointed out in his introduction, the problem then was not that modern architecture had to be learnt, but that a deal of unlearning of conventional habits must go on. In the last 20 years of this century architects again need to recall the energy and ideas which generated the milieu from which we practice. Functionalism, with its attendant distrust of historical exemplars, appears now as a reductive doctrine, yet at the time McGrath was writing, it was the Occam's razor that cut through tradition and habit. With the obsession with styling that is now de rigueur, the architectural fraternity – more international than ever – has lost the diagrammatic clarity of those earlier times. As convinced a historicist as Philip Johnson has commented that the newest architecture has nothing new to offer in planning terms. Equally, however, there can be no reason for this, unless – with the advent of cheaper colour photographic reproduction – pictures have taken over from real drawings, while drawing has come to mean a sketch of a picture.

The abstract nature of plan drawings raises the issue of invention versus convention, at the widest level. If there is invention, for whatever reasons, then it will be evident in the plan – or, in some cases such as Loos, in the section. What is new is not the style or look of the building but the underlying structure (which is the plan) that generates the building. Materials play an essential role, but materials alone can only generate a new style (this surely is the lesson of Art Nouveau).

In most of the buildings, two kinds of plan appear. The first zones the plan either vertically and/or horizontally, and the second tries to abolish separate rooms altogether to
2 produce a truly free plan, finally achieved in the Farnsworth House by Mies van der Rohe.

Between these two kinds of plan there are many variations, variations which even when assembled in such a small number as we have here, show the range and fertility of the discourse within modern architecture. A discourse it must be, because a variety of ideas are exchanged and seem to be in the air, and communication occurred more through pictorial imagery than words.

But once the basic terms of this drawn discourse of modern architecture were established, which had occurred by the time the movement became codified in Yorke, Hitchcock and Johnson, and McGrath, a new vernacular based upon the variations arose. For there now to be an increase in invention, metaphors had to be brought into play; and the materials of the traditional architecture, especially brick, could be used without the historicist overtones that they might have had in the 20s. Amancio Williams' house is a bridge, over not a raging torrent but a small stream, which therefore makes the metaphorical nature of the section obvious. Goldfinger's house in Hampstead, London may have been brick because that material was cheap, but he could use brick without its traditional associations by the end of the 30s.

If, by 1945, something akin to a vernacular of modern architecture existed, then new conventions arose. And once this happened, kinds of plans could be interpreted as types, and these types could be construed as a typology, and that typology advertised a historian's category – Modernism. Later 'Modernism' would be attacked, because a movement that had stretched across continents was made a simple catchword, and a catch-all for the ills of society. Upon this groundwork the patent non-sequitur of 'post-modernism' could be used as a category. In other arts that term designated something new, in painting the work of the New York school, especially Jasper Johns, and in literature the work of Bartelme, Ishmael Read and others. As a label, post-modernism has a singularly American provenance. But in architecture, there is no such thing as a post-modern plan, and what passes for such work relies upon the homely clichés of the end of the 19th century.

The plan of a building, therefore, is the most accurate measure we have of changes in architectural thought since the Beaux Arts. Recent experience of the post-modern brouhaha could have this conclusion as its epitaph. Architects should be reminded of the techniques of drawing and representation, which are their single most particular skill, when they are confronted with the crude historicist facadism of much currently published work. Plans are the result of a process which involves criticism and self-criticism. Both forms of criticism entail some dialogue between the eye and what is drawn on paper. Words need be neither spoken nor thought. The concepts in play need only be graphic or architectural. Post-modernism deals entirely with literal images which need words in order for the symbols to make sense. A plan needs none, and while drawing it the architect is simultaneously in contact with abstractions and a potential reality. A history of architecture, or even a history of building, needs this representation in order to tie it closely to the order of work which produces the discourse, of which any one plan is but a small component. Words themselves are totally unsatisfactory descriptions of architecture.

This book is the result of a corporate effort. While it carries no dedication, I would like to express my thanks to my colleague, Jon Corpe, for whom teaching and working are inseparable activities.

David Dunster
London, September 1984

EDWIN LUTYENS: Homewood

1901

Lutyens (1869-1944) built Homewood at Kneb-worth, Hertfordshire for his mother-in-law, the Dowager, Countess of Lytton. It is a four-square elm-boarded house set on a brick base, with classical elements in the entrance and the garden side coyly advancing themselves from behind the skirts of a made-up vernacular.

In the planning, a slight swerve off axis allows Lutyens to arrange both the main room to the south-east and the staircase hall facing south-west so that each aligns with large but simply planned lawns. Desiring axiality overall and in the major rooms has the consequence that minor rooms and service corridors become contorted and awkward. It is no accident that corridors at Homewood exist only in the servants' quarter (to the north) of the plan, while the owners and their guests promenade from room to room. There is evidence that Lutyens was conscious of this, as the section at Homewood shows.

Many of his houses were long and thin, present-ing no internal lighting difficulties. Homewood was nearly square in plan, and Lutyens had the problem of how to light the centre of the plan. He

Ground floor plan

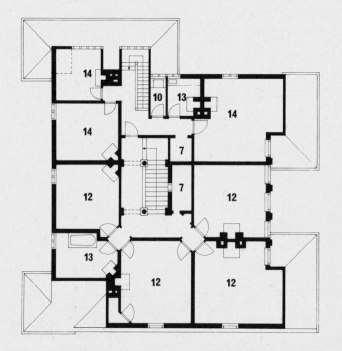

First floor plan

1 Vestibule	8 Pantry
2 Hall	9 Kitchen
3 Drawing room	10 WC
4 Dining room	11 Scullery
5 Study	12 Bedroom
6 Servants' hall	13 Bathroom
7 Store	14 Servants

4

achieved this – much as he had done at Tigbourne Court (1899), and as he would again in The Salutation (1911) – by taking the staircase across the plan on the opposite axis to that of the entrance, and then lighting the first floor staircase landing from above.

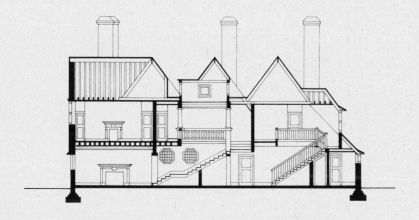

Section

Garden front

FRANK LLOYD WRIGHT: Robie House

1909

Frank Lloyd Wright (1867-1959) built this house in the then-prosperous district near the University of Chicago. His client and he appeared to be in total accord, and the house cost $1000 less than estimated. Clearly it required servants, for the entrance hall is only accessible from the garage, and that implies that visitors and guests arrived in chauffeur-driven cars.

Wright and the client wanted to get away from large entrance halls, and from the cluttered spaces of Chicago planning. Not unusually, however, the living and dining rooms are on the upper floor, with the eaves and terraces extending above street level into space.

Fine Roman brickwork is the basic material, with stone cappings to walls and a complexly structured overhanging low-pitched roof.

The linear first floor ties together the living and dining rooms, which are separated by a massive sculptural fireplace and staircase. The plan relies on the lower ceiling height next to the continuous window band, with the central space being higher in the living room, establishing some hierarchy in the volumetric length.

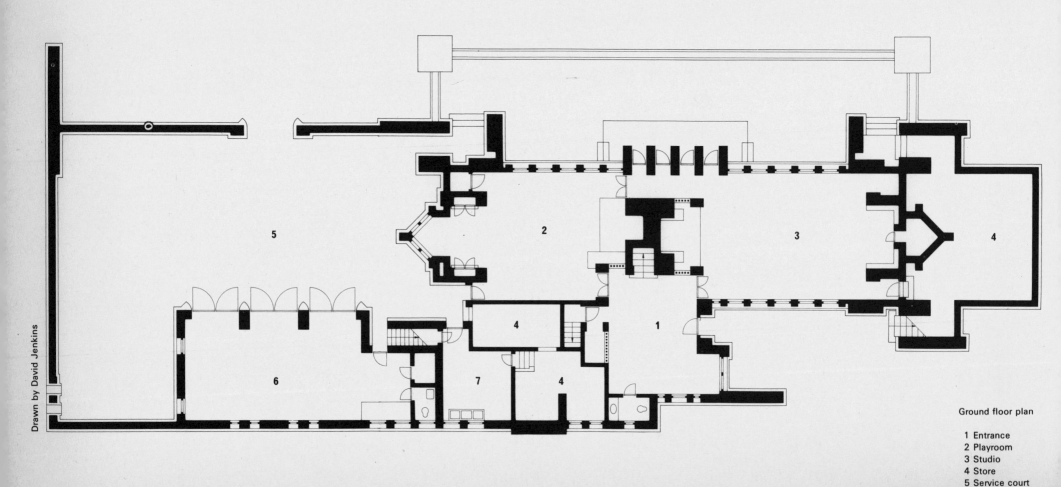

Drawn by David Jenkins

Ground floor plan

1 Entrance
2 Playroom
3 Studio
4 Store
5 Service court
6 Garage
7 Laundry

Living room terrace

Street elevation

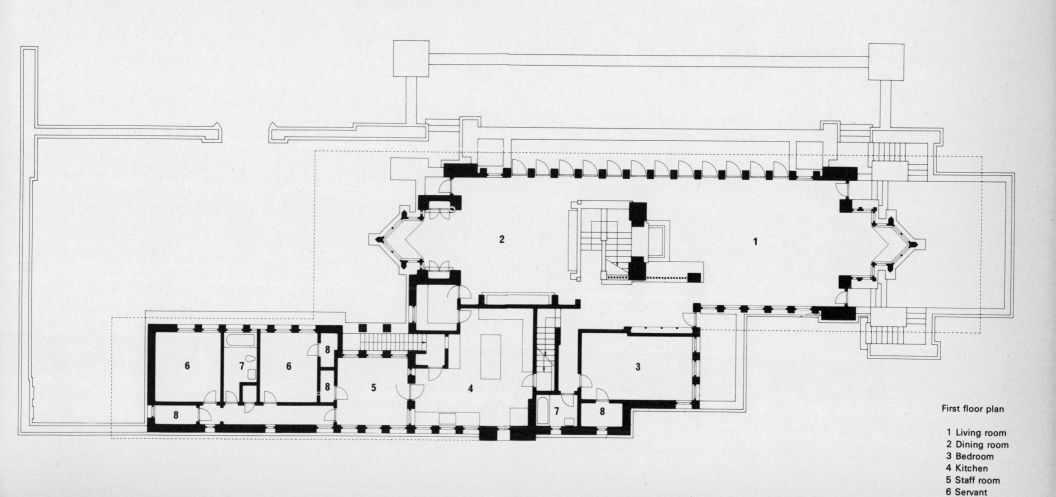

First floor plan

1 Living room
2 Dining room
3 Bedroom
4 Kitchen
5 Staff room
6 Servant
7 Bathroom
8 Store

JOSEF HOFFMANN : Palais Stoclet
1911

The building is in Woluwe St Pierre, a wealthy suburb of Brussels. The clients were the Stoclets, rich and highly cultured. They chose Hoffmann to build them a house when they lived in Vienna, but returned to Brussels on the death of Stoclet père, keeping Hoffmann as architect.

Hoffmann (1870-1956) worked on the building from 1905 for six years, in complete control of every detail. The interiors were made by members of the Wiener Werkstätte and follow no clear iconographic programme. The load-bearing brick walls are covered externally by a thin veneer of Norwegian white marble edged in gilt and dull metal.

On the ground floor are all public spaces, a small concert room, main hall, study, eating

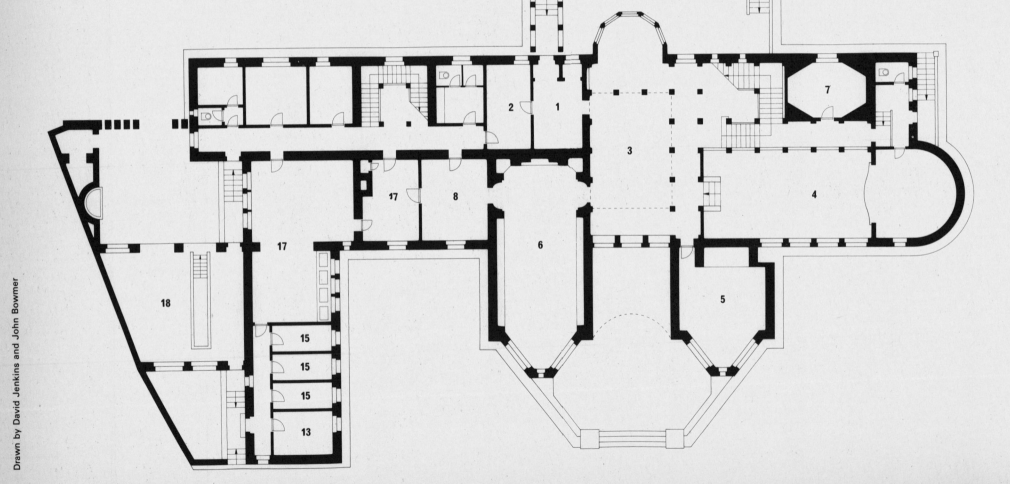

Ground floor plan

rooms, and a service wing to the right. The first floor has sleeping accommodation for the family, with servants' and guest rooms on the floor above. In this sense the house is a conventional 19th-century organization. The decoration of rooms with strong alternating sequences of low to high, light to dark spaces is also 19th-century in its evocation of character as the concept of generating a plan. But because eclectic ornament was generally suppressed, the house was seen by contemporaries as the harbinger of a new style.

For further information see E F Sekler: 'The Stoclet House by Josef Hoffmann' in 'Essays in the History of Architecture Presented to R Wittkower', Phaidon, New York and London, 1967.

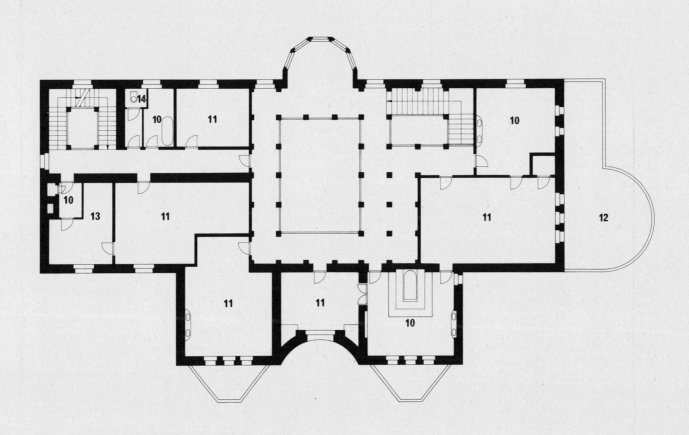

1 Entrance
2 Cloaks
3 Hall
4 Music room
5 M Stoclet's room
6 Dining room
7 Sitting room
8 Breakfast room
9 Void
10 Bathroom
11 Bedroom
12 Balcony
13 Servant's room
14 WC
15 Store
16 Guest room
17 Kitchen
18 Garage

First floor plan

Palais Stoclet

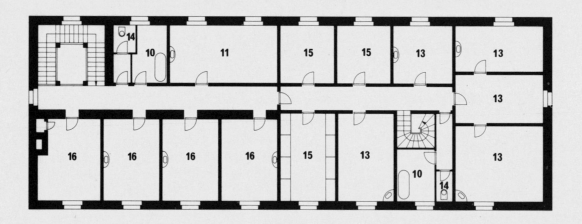

Second floor plan

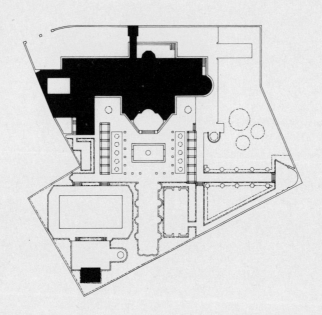

Site plan

HECTOR GUIMARD: Hotel Guimard
1912

Hector Guimard (1867-1942) built his own house in the 16th arrondissement which became his territory in Paris. His masterpiece, the Castel Béranger, is not far away. He completed the house by the age of 45, but his career was never to reach the success he enjoyed before World War I. His adoption of Viollet le Duc's principles was to leave him wedded to expressive forms of construction, modelled on Gothic architecture that would be rejected within ten years of the completion of this house.

His major problem on the main floor was to include two oval living rooms arranged en suite, on an extremely awkward triangular site. His office occupied the ground floor, with the main floor of living rooms over that. The master bedroom is on the second floor, and above that a studio for his wife, with a guest room. In order for each floor to have a different spatial character, the staircase is squeezed into a triangular corner on the main street facade. Mirrors are used there, in the manner of Victor Horta, to extend a very narrow but surprisingly well-lit space.

On the facade, three symmetries order the wall

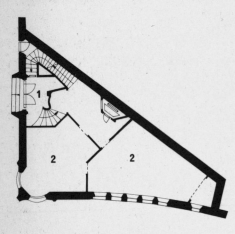

Ground floor plan

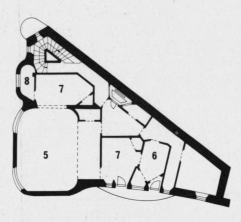

Second floor plan

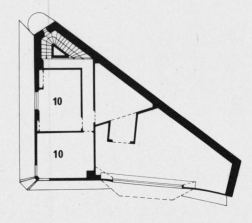

Fourth floor plan

First floor plan

Third floor plan

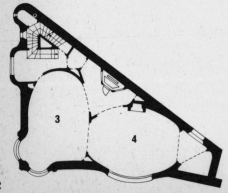

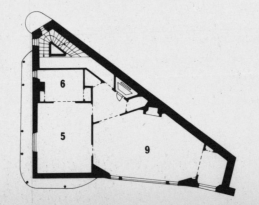

Drawn by Lucia Mortato

1 Entrance
2 Office
3 Dining room
4 Living room
5 Bedroom
6 Bathroom
7 Dressing room
8 WC
9 Studio
10 Servant

12

planes. All run from ground to roof and appear to widen as they turn from the vertical symmetry over the door, to the corner bay, and then to the widest facade, crowned by a big north-facing window for his wife's painting studio. Materials are brick and stone externally, with plaster inside in most rooms to make the wall surface appear to bend over to make the ceiling plane.

Living room

GUNNAR ASPLUND: Villa Snellman
1918

Asplund (1885-1940) completed this building in the suburb of Djursholm, near Stockholm, two years before he began work on his best known building, the Public Library in Stockholm. That most austere neo-classical exercise can be juxtaposed with the more personal and rustic simplicity of this house, its decoration limited to a few swags.

The house is approached up a wide set of steps onto a terrace. From this, a pair of solid doors and a pair of glazed doors lead into the house and establish a winter and a summer entrance. Inside, the rooms are connected by a neat trompe l'oeil corridor. The skew angle of this corridor is a typical device, similar to the way the service wing is connected to the main body of the building. The

eye corrects both these distortions, so why did Asplund introduce them? And why do the windows of the back elevation slide so mysteriously out of alignment?

Surely there are functional answers to these questions, but the consistent trickery of Asplund suggests that it was perception itself that he wished to play with.

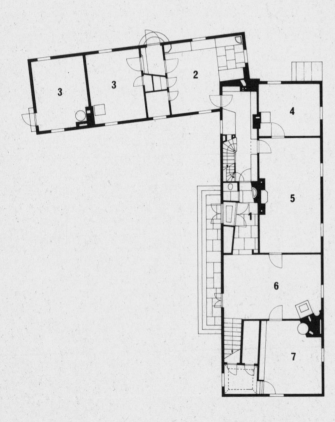

Ground floor plan

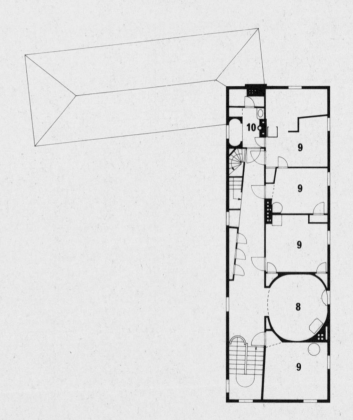

First floor plan

Drawn by Mike Russum

1 Entrance
2 Kitchen
3 Servant
4 Sitting room
5 Dining
6 Living room
7 Study
8 Hall
9 Bedroom
10 Bathroom

Back elevation   Front elevation

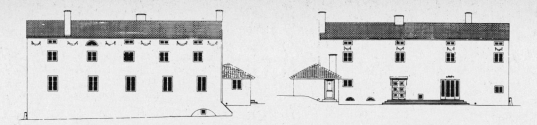

Front door (winter)

Section

Entrance court

First floor hall

First floor corridor

15

RUDOLF SCHINDLER: Schindler & Chase Houses

1922

Rudolf Schindler (1887-1953) trained in Vienna, emigrated to America to work for Frank Lloyd Wright, and settled in Los Angeles where he became part of the left-wing avant-garde.

He and his wife occupied this house until their deaths. Schindler who considered it a masterpiece wrote: 'The distinction between indoors and outdoors will disappear. Our house will lose its front and back door aspect. . .each individual will want a private room to gain a background for his sleep.' The two families would share a common kitchen, and while each member possessed a private room, they were expected in the southern California climate to sleep more healthily on outdoor porches. Thus this house advocates a totally different way of life from that of the conventional Victorian dwelling.

The house was built very cheaply and with the simplest apparatus. Wall slabs were cast on site, flat, then lifted into place. Between these wall slabs are narrow strips of glass. The roof construction and sliding doors are timber.

The house is currently in the hands of a trust which aims to return it to its former state.

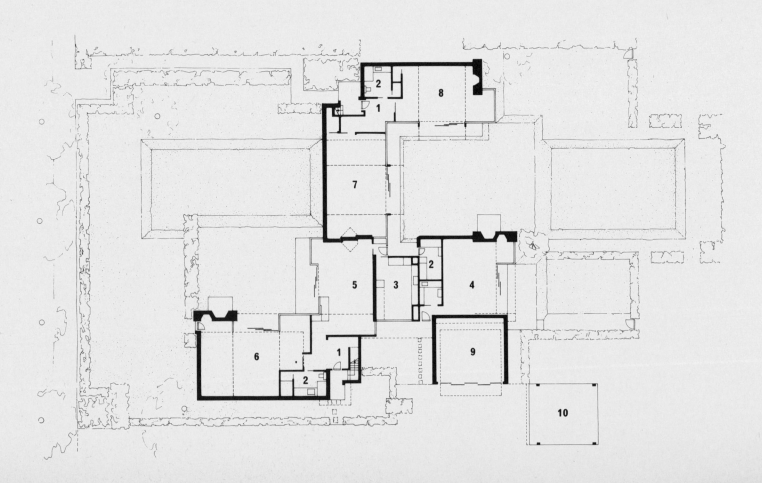

Drawn by Richard Porchmouth

Ground floor plan

1 Hall
2 Bathroom
3 Kitchen
4 Guestroom
5 Mrs Chase's room
6 Mr Chase's room
7 Mrs Schindler's room
8 Mr Schindler's room
9 Garage
10 Carport

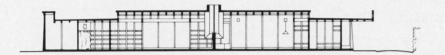

Long section

View of a courtyard

JJP OUD
1923

This small hut shows Oud's (1890-1963) work in a transitional phase between the influence of Berlage and the emerging De Stijl movement. At this time Oud was working with van Doesberg and the painter, Kammerlingh Onnes, as well as absorbing the influence through the Wasmuth publications of Frank Lloyd Wright. What changed his work was the idea of new construction methods and materials and the possibility of new ways of living, all of which he experimented with when he undertook housing work in Rotterdam.

The hut was built as a superintendent's office, and while not strictly a house it could easily be transformed into a weekend retreat. The fireplace on the axis of the house is lined with tiles and has a slit window where a flue would normally be expected. The smoke rose to a ventilator in the flat roof. Light entered the central corridor through the light-box on the roof, glazed on four sides.

In his later work he became more of a functionalist, but never lost the playfulness inherent in this temporary building.

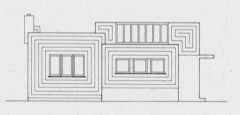

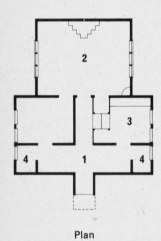

Plan

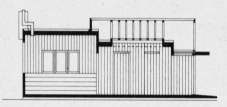

Long elevation

Section through main room + entrance

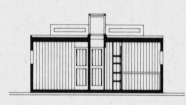

Section through kitchen

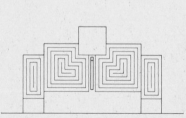

External elevation of fire-place wall

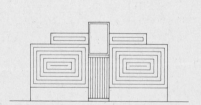

Entrance elevation

1 Entrance
2 Main room
3 Kitchen
4 Bathroom

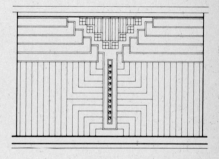

Fireplace

BIJVOET & DUIKER: House at Aalsmeer

1924

In their house for a master gardener in a village near the Zuider Zee, Bernard Bijvoet (1889-?) and Johannes Duiker (1890-1935) adopted a local vernacular form of construction, a timber frame covered in close boarding. The circular staircase tower is covered in shingles. As Robert Vickery points out in his article on the partnership in Yale 'Perspecta' 13/14, this form of construction allowed windows to appear on the facade in long banks, and to pass around corners, giving the impression of weightlessness which characterized De Stijl architecture.

In the planning there is little wasted space: each room has radically different proportions and the services and circulation are squeezed to minimum sizes. The expression of this planning effort on the facades is explicit. The pitches of the roofs, window shapes, and projections and recessions suggest the functional expressionism of the post-war era, which would also adopt the mono-pitch roof forms but from the different source of Scandinavian and Danish housing.

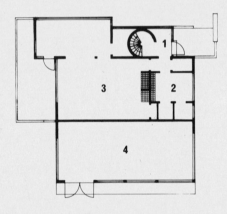

Ground floor plan

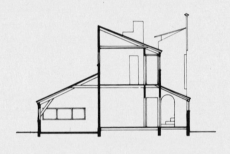

Section through greenhouse

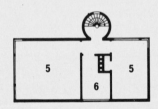

First floor plan

Long section

1 Entrance
2 Kitchen
3 Living room
4 Greenhouse
5 Bedroom
6 Bathroom

Drawn by Paul Gregory

20

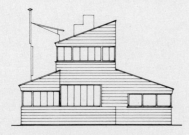

Back elevation

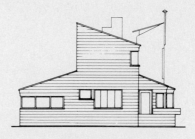

Entrance elevation

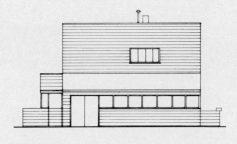

Greenhouse elevation

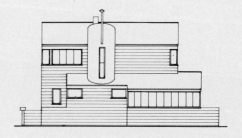

Side elevation

AUGUSTE PERRET: House at Versailles

1924

Perret's (1874-1954) design appears symmetrical on the short facade, but only the upper level is in close symmetry. The ground floor entrance leads straight into a studio; the house was built for a painter, Calliandre. This room causes the ground floor to have the build-up of masses (and cornices) which Le Corbusier had used in his Villa Schwab of 1916.

The front of the house is lower, and the two bedrooms either side of the staircase landing are reached by two separate short flights. The staircase continues in a volume that protrudes from the back, higher part of the house.

Perret opposed Le Corbusier's idea of long horizontal bands of windows; he aligned the windows vertically, in the tradition of classicism.

His pared-down elevations begin to have some feeling of Roman weight, which surfaced again in the work of Louis Kahn. Perret's incipient modernism of the Théâtre du Champs Elysées was diluted here, as he stepped back towards the traditional plan of the house, where only the section and elevations recall his pioneering earlier work.

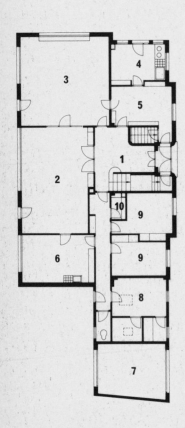

Drawn by David Jenkins

Ground floor plan

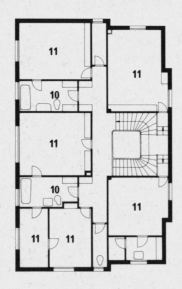

First floor plan

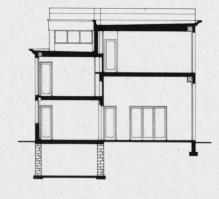

Section through studio

1 Entrance
2 Studio
3 Living room
4 Kitchen
5 Office
6 Store
7 Garage
8 Laundry
9 Servant
10 Bathroom
11 Bedroom

Garden front

GERRIT RIETVELD: Schröder-Schräder House

1924

Gerrit Rietveld (1884-1964) worked closely in collaboration with the client for this house. More than any other, this is either – in Banham's words – 'a cardboard Mondrian' or an enormous piece of furniture masquerading as a house. All windows could only be opened up completely, at right angles to frames, repeating the devices by which the upper floor could be transformed from one single space into a series of smaller ones – the point being that in either positioning of windows or moveable walls, the house retained its neo-plastic hypothesis.

The house, anchored to the end lot of a series of more conventional Utrecht housing, has neither a background nor foreground in its composition. The plan has certainly been ignored in favour of its three facades, but each window specifically relates to the space behind and must have given good views before the motorway was built.

Like so many experimental paths taken in the 1920s, this house was an end-point suggesting no way forward.

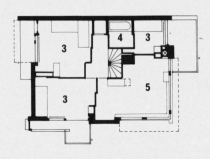

Ground floor plan

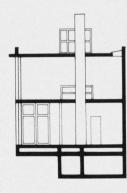

First floor plan – partitions closed

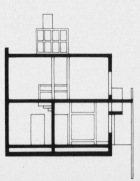

Section through fire-place

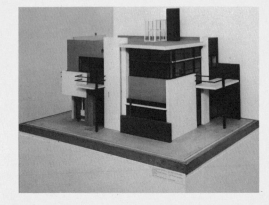

Model

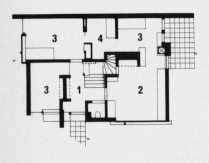

Drawn by Heidi Löcker

First floor plan – partitions open

1 Entrance
2 Kitchen
3 Bedroom
4 Bathroom
5 Living room

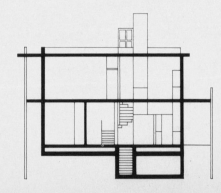

Section through living-space

Long section

Garden side

LE CORBUSIER: Mother's House
1924

The site, a long thin strip between a road and Lake Geneva, would necessarily produce a long thin house. Le Corbusier (1887-1965) turns the problem to advantage and diagrammatically inserts within the long rectangle of the plan only one partition assembly of walls. This effectively divides the space in a manner analogous to the positioning of the service core in the Farnsworth House by Mies van der Rohe, completed 24 years later.

The house, built of concrete blocks, was finally completely sheathed in aluminium sheeting; it has a roof terrace, a ship window 11 metres long to the lake, and an expressionist way of placing both a boiler and a sink outside the main enclosure. There is little thought of repeating this design, nor of advertising it as an exemplar of his five points.

Nonetheless it is the only house to which he devoted a book, 'Une Petite Maison', and the attention to detail was all that could be expected of a doting son.

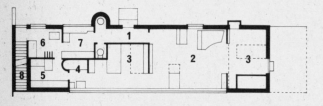

Floor plan

1 Entrance
2 Living room
3 Bedroom
4 Bathroom
5 Kitchen
6 Store
7 Laundry
8 Stairs

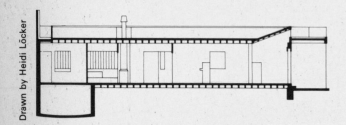

Drawn by Heidi Löcker

Long section

Entrance side

26

LE CORBUSIER: Ternisien House
1926

Built close by the Lipschitz-Metschianinoff houses in Boulogne Bilancourt, in the suburbs of Paris, this very small house combines many programmatic themes of the manifesto days of l'Esprit Nouveau. Entry is between a cubic solid and a curving wall, and the house divides into two parts. In the cube was the studio and bedroom, and in the triangular space the living room. The entrance hall opened into the kitchen and dining room, and over this a covered terrace made that entrance more imposing. From the first floor terrace access could also be gained to the roof of the studio/bedroom cube.

Like his mother's house completed two years earlier, a difficult site engendered more invention and clarity than his larger houses did. If he allowed any metaphorical play it was to bring the drain of the upper terrace to the sharp point of the triangle and expose it as a 'column', the only one in the building. By a paradox of fate this small corner device is all that remains of M Ternisien's house, which has now been replaced by a crude art deco apartment building.

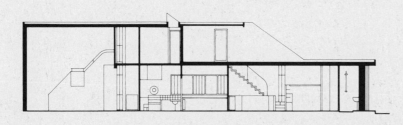

Long section

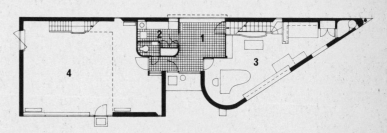

Ground floor plan

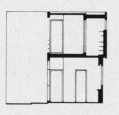

Section through entrance

Section through studio

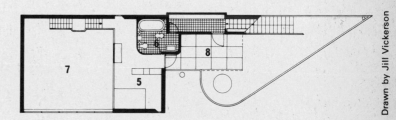

First floor plan

Drawn by Jill Vickerson

1 Entrance
2 Kitchen
3 Living room
4 Studio
5 Bedroom
6 Bathroom
7 Void
8 Roof terrace

WALTER GROPIUS: Double House

1926

Of the buildings Gropius (1883-1969) designed for the Bauhaus premises, the houses in Dessau in the DDR are the most restrained. Sharp, cubic, with balconies at first floor level, they are rooted to their sites as a deliberate contrast to the surrounding landscape. The porte-cochère of his own house is abandoned, and the two houses have little that is monumental about them, as his own did. The plan organization is identical, with one a 90° rotated version of the other. This allows both houses similar views and sun penetration.

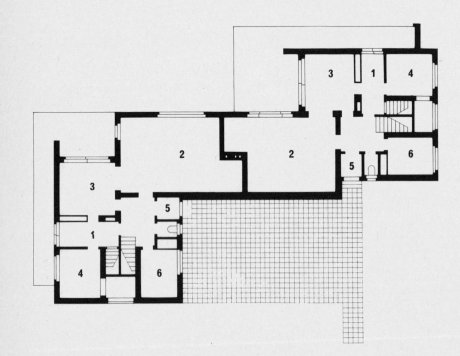

Drawn by Heidi Löcker

Ground floor plan

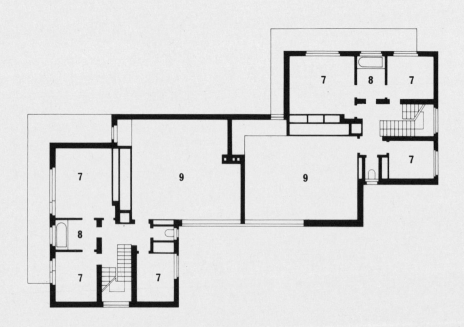

First floor plan

1 Entrance
2 Living room
3 Dining room
4 Kitchen
5 Store
6 Maid's room
7 Bedroom
8 Bathroom
9 Studio

General view

RICHARD NEUTRA: Health House
1926

Built for the same client, Dr Lovell, as Schindler's Newport Beach House of 1926, Neutra's house sits in a valley just across from Frank Lloyd Wright's Ennis House of 1924. A steel frame structure consistently punctuates the plan, whose exterior is infilled with cement spandrel or steel panels. This is why, when it was built, it became so famous. Yet from the outside it looks very little like the systems buildings of the 1960s.

The top floor is for bedrooms, each with its own outdoor sleeping porch, an obsession with Lovell. The long fully-glazed living room below extends back into the hillside, cut to form a terrace, with service rooms lined up behind on the same floor. Below this is another terrace and swimming pool There is little coordination of vertical service runs.

The house has weathered well, looked after by Neutra and his clients. It made his name in America and Europe.

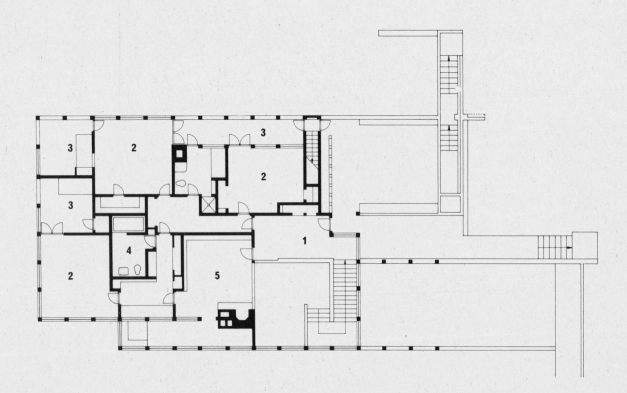

Drawn by David Jenkins

Second floor plan

Living room

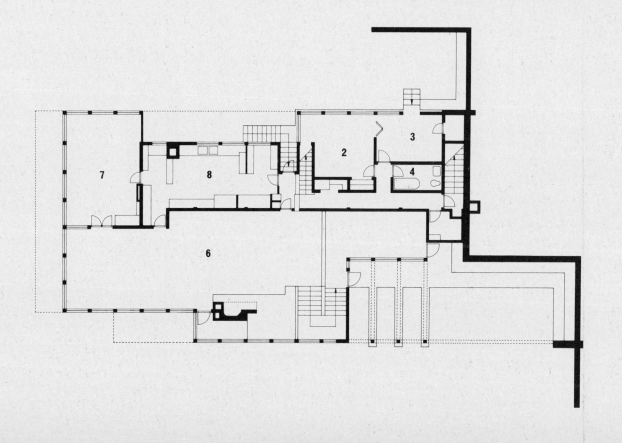

First floor plan

1 Entrance
2 Bedroom
3 Sleeping balcony
4 Bathroom
5 Sitting room
6 Living room
7 Dining room
8 Kitchen
9 Store
10 Pool

Health House

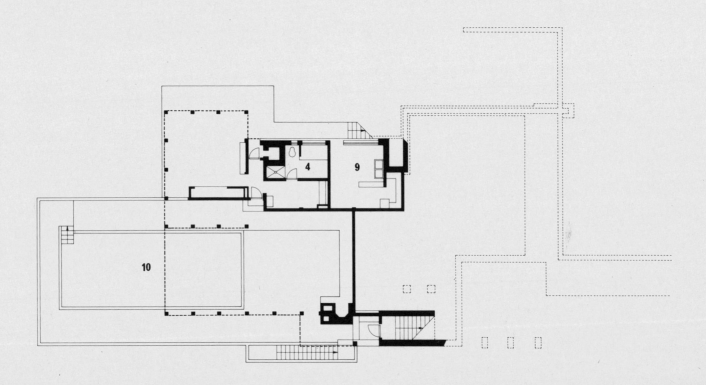

Ground floor plan

L DE KONINCK: Villa Lenglet
1926

De Koninck (b.1896) built this studio house in le Loclet, Belgium for a painter. Originally to be in reinforced concrete, it was built using a concrete frame and rendered concrete blocks. It clearly is a pure modern movement house with 'existenz-minimum' in mind. Apart from the staircase in the double-height living room, there is barely 4 square metres of circulation space in the house.

In terms of the planning it looks like a hybrid developed from Rietveld's Schröder-Schräder houses of 1924 and Le Corbusier's houses for artisans. With Rietveld it shares a plan with a staircase rising in the centre to a room as large as the entire house; and with Le Corbusier's project it shares a roof which drains to a central column attached to that staircase.

Robert Delevoy remarks that De Koninck worked with two ideas: 'a model of architecture without an architect' – vernacular Belgian farm housing: and an idea of serialized industrial building. His inventions include a glass brick, an industrialized kitchen, and at least two industrialized construction systems. His interest in anonymity is clear from his detailing in primary 'purist' forms.

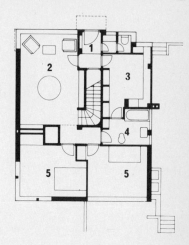

Ground floor plan

Street elevation

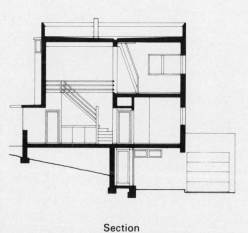

Section

1 Entrance
2 Living room
3 Kitchen
4 Bathroom
5 Bedroom
6 void
7 Studio

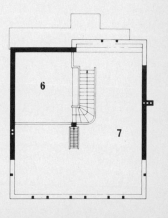

First floor plan

Drawn by Bob Dye

33

LE CORBUSIER: Villa Stein
1927

The structure of this house is a reinforced concrete frame arranged in a wide/narrow bay rhythm across the width of the site. The narrow bays generally indicate circulation and service zones. The front and back facades of the house are cantilevered from the main frame and appear as pure planes, with the back facade being close to an inversion of the frontal facade in terms of its horizontal pattern of solid to void.

Internally the plan retains little of the architectural promenade that characterized the early projects; it becomes a variation on the L-shaped plan and section of the Immeuble Villa project.

The house was built for the Stein family, but their furnishings were never to the architect's taste. The system of roof terraces which open from the roof and cascade down to the garden is perhaps the most exciting formal invention. The internal spaces, by contrast, appear vast and curiously dull. The problem of furnishing living spaces was one which Le Corbusier never really faced up to, except in his much smaller houses where furniture was much more like small moveable pieces of equipment. The living room of the

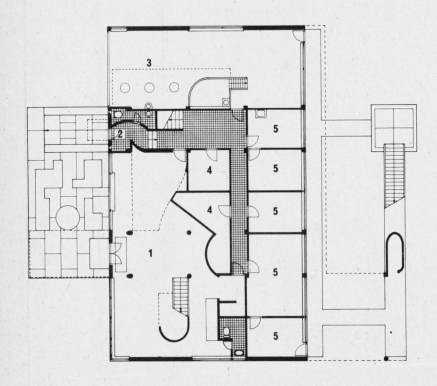

Ground floor plan

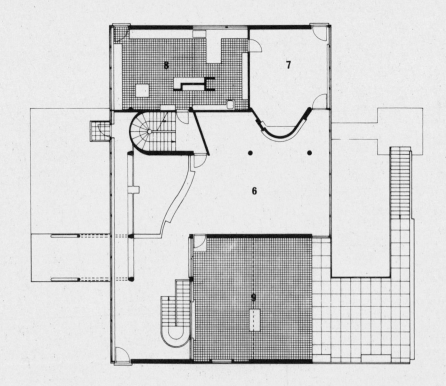

First floor plan

Drawn by Simon Colebrook

1 Entrance hall	6 Living room
2 Service entrance	7 Dining room
3 Garage	8 Kitchen
4 Store	9 Terrace
5 Servant	

Villa Stein, like that of the Ville Savoie, is waiting for the installation of an exhibition of primitive sculpture rather than chairs and tables suitable for family use. The sculptural adjustments of the dining room curve and the 'writing desk' over the only double-height space are swamped by the monumental scale of the interior.

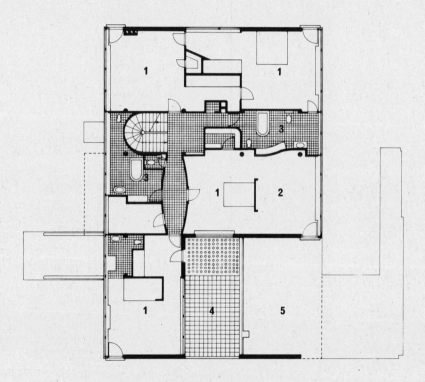

Second floor plan

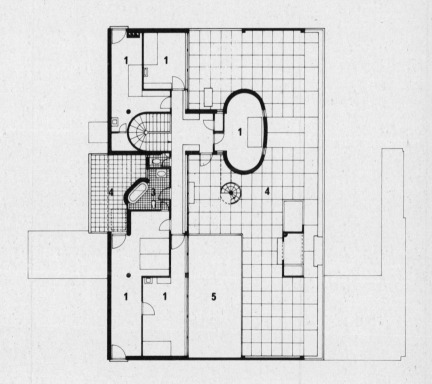

Third floor plan

1 Bedroom
2 Dressing room
3 Bathroom
4 Roof terrace
5 Void

Villa Stein

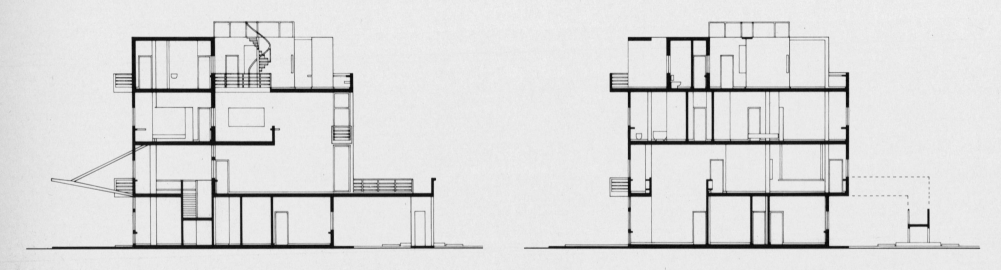

Sections

Garden elevation

Front elevation

37

WALTER GROPIUS: Dessau

1927

By 1926 Gropius had completed the Bauhaus buildings and the professors' housing there. At Törten he put into practice his ideas about industrialized mass housing, of which these were the earliest plans. The entire site was laid out during the construction according to his designs. Walls of the houses are concrete block; concrete lintel/beams spanning between front and back were hoisted into position by crane. Floors and roofs were installed, followed by the windows which were screwed up to the concrete lintels. All services are on the surface; the outside has the infill panels painted, but the concrete structure left exposed. Glass bricks surround the entrance door.

From the entrance hall, to one side is the living room, and straight ahead the living kitchen in which meals were eaten. The kitchen also contained a bath, and looks as if it was laid out in accordance with the 'scientific' principles of household management which had already found expression in Ernst May's New Frankfurt. The water closet was in this version still outside the house, in the extension into the garden.

Drawn by Geraldine Walder

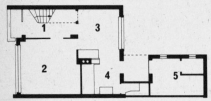

Ground floor plan

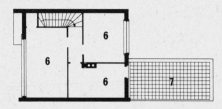

First floor plan

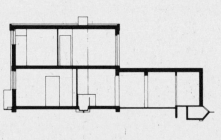

Long section

1 Entrance
2 Living room
3 Dining room
4 Kitchen
5 Bathroom
6 Bedroom
7 Terrace

In these industrially conceived houses, the rationales of functionalism were explicitly laid out. Minimal space standards produced the size of rooms which have now become internationally enshrined in housing statutes. The kitchen was the only innovation in planning terms.

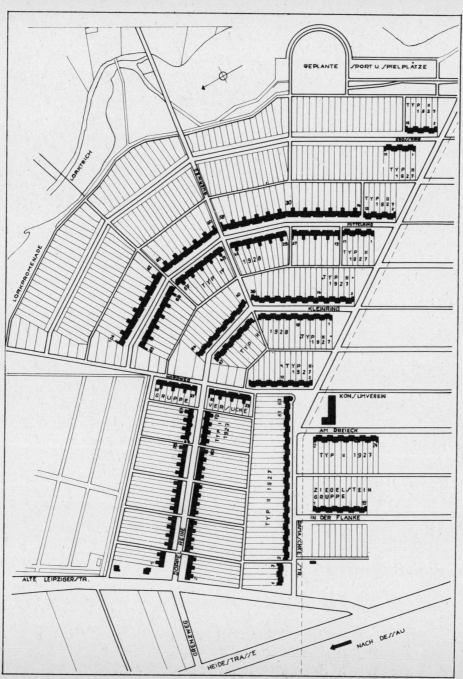

KONSTANTIN MELNIKOV: Own House
1927

Melnikov (1890-1974) built this house for himself in Moscow at a time when the New Economic Policy in Russia was encouraging private initiative in a number of ways. It was damaged during World War II but rebuilt. The architect lived in it throughout his life.

The formal idea of two interlocking cylinders occurs many times in Melnikov's work. The construction of this house is very crude brickwork rendered over. All openings are made from corbelling the bricks so that there are neither lintels nor conventional sills. Floors are a timber egg-crate construction. The house was extremely cheap and drew upon unsophisticated building labour and what materials were to hand.

Melnikov wanted the house to be light and airy.

Originally the bedrooms were faced in thin stone sheets to make them dust-free as well, so that after sleeping the occupant would rise completely refreshed to carry on the revolution. The living spaces, however, became unsatisfactory in use because all vertical circulation occurs through them. The house is a remarkable personal statement of its or any time.

Ground floor plan

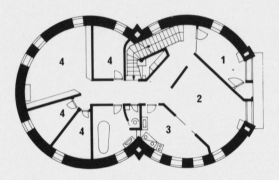

Second floor plan

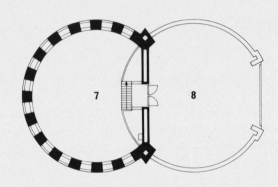

Section

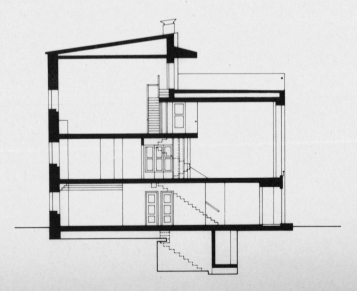

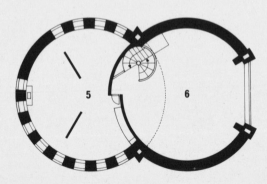

First floor plan

1 Entrance
2 Dining room
3 Kitchen
4 Store
5 Bedroom
6 Living room
7 Studio
8 Terrace

Building under construction

Street elevation

MART STAM: Houses at Weissenhof

1927

Stam's (1899-?) built work is limited in the west, where he is known as the designer of the cantilevered steel tube chair and co-author of the Van Nelle factory. For one so involved in the polemics of the time, these three houses are the most well-known single work. While they were the cheapest houses to rent in cost per square metre, in area and volume they were quite large compared to other Weissenhof Siedlung projects.

Oriented to the sun and view, with one very large living room, these three-bedroom houses have the most reduced and refined plans. If there are any 'architectural' devices, they are related to staircases. In two houses a staircase leads down to a garden level workroom; all three houses have one room for a live-in servant, lit indirectly across the stairwell.

Stam did not believe in built-in furniture, unlike many modern movement contemporaries. He saw – like Hannes Meyer – a direct link between economics and building. He wrote in 'Wie Bauen?' (How to Build): 'Man must abandon traditional ways of living in favour of a more economical way of life for his own sake. He must learn to renounce

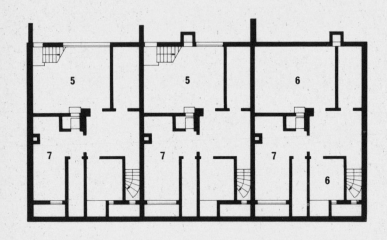

Basement

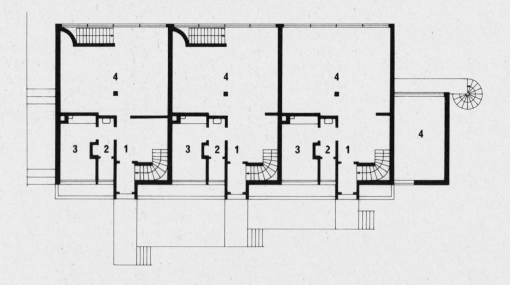

Ground floor plan

1 Entrance
2 WC
3 Kitchen
4 Living room
5 Basement room
6 Store
7 Boiler
8 Bedroom
9 Bathroom
10 Maid's room
11 Roof terrace

any desire for representational character, he must accustom himself to another measure of value than that of a wide house front and the use of expensive materials. He must restrict his demands, but despite this he has the right to equal cost of dwellings, maximum usefulness and an increased convenience.'

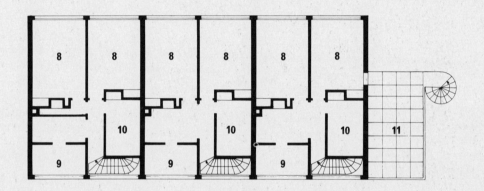

First floor plan

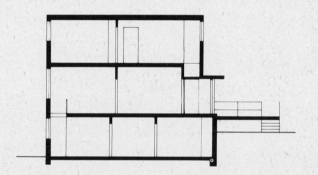

Section

LUCKHARDT BROTHERS: House at Rupenhorn

1928

Three single-family houses were proposed in echelon on the site by the Luckhardts (Wassili, 1889-1972, Hans, 1890-1954). Two were completed, consisting of a lightweight steel frame for walls and floors, infilled with panels. The erection process above foundations was dry, except for the thin coat of finishing render inside and out.

Service rooms occupy the ground floor and a large first floor terrace swings out over the garage below. A large living room occupies the first floor and is fully glazed to the south. Bedrooms are on the floors above, and there is a roof terrace.

Industrialized components were ingeniously used during the experimental 1920s. Each of these three houses looked quite different but each was constructed in an identical system.

Formal antecedents sometimes take over from reason. The entrance is on the narrow flank close to the back of the house, signalled by a split between the wall planes coming together at the corner. As at the Villa Stein, this split is glazed over four floors. Small protruding balconies lead out from a service room, a maid's room, which is justifiable, and on the upmost level, a store: the

Ground floor plan

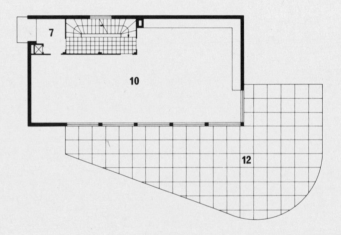

First floor plan

Drawn by Mike Emptage

1 Entrance
2 Kitchen
3 Servant
4 Bathroom
5 WC
6 Laundry
7 Store
8 Boiler
9 Garage
10 Living room
11 Bedroom
12 Terrace

expressive gesture is hardly fully justified.

Nonetheless the interiors have a quiet calm. This calmness became the trademark of Berlin architects' work at this time, in contrast to the more self-proclaiming interiors found in France. The cupboards flush with the wall surface, ordered shelves, and formal sitting layouts indicate the continued formality of German middle-class life.

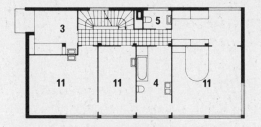

Second floor plan

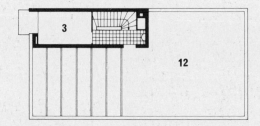
Third floor plan

Garden elevation

45

MIES VAN DER ROHE: Lange House

1928

Now the Municipal Museum of Modern Art at Krefeld, and adjacent to the sister house for the Esters family, is the last of Mies's (1886-1969) essays in brickwork. It is a very large house in which his planning techniques hover between the traditional plans of the time and the free-planning idea which matured at the Tugendhat House. To the left of the entrance is the service side with a

lower ground floor garage. The bedrooms are accessed from a lower corridor and open onto a terrace. The house is zoned for use by floors.

According to Hitchcock, the client required a traditional looking house; but in this villa suburb, however restrained it is, the house is far from traditional. The blue/brown brick is the only concession. Mies handled the material as if it

composed a sculptured mass. Whether it is structural or not does not seem to matter. The brick lintel over the entrance door returns on the reveal of the soffit, where the bricks are effectively suspended.

On the garden side, the vast covered outdoor room has marble slabs cantilevered from it for sculpture, and the brickwork continues as steps

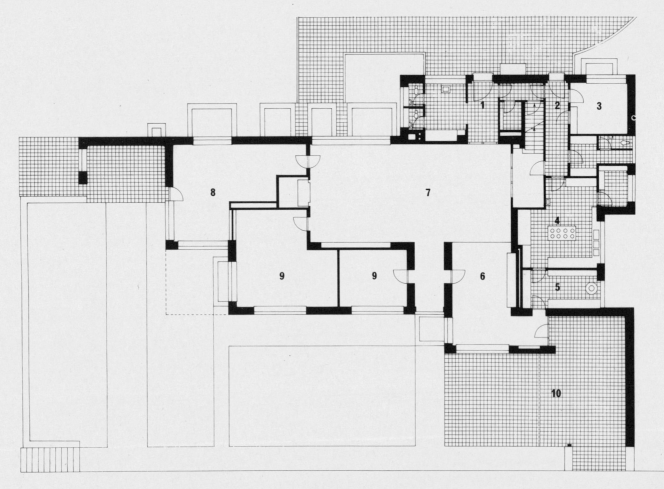

Drawn by Mike Russum

Ground floor plan

1 Entrance
2 Service entrance
3 Maid's room
4 Kitchen
5 Servery
6 Dining room
7 Living room
8 Study
9 Day room
10 Covered terrace
11 Bedroom
12 Bathroom
13 Store
14 Laundry

down to an 'English' garden. Like Mies's later American work, the house leaves a clear impression of another successful experiment.

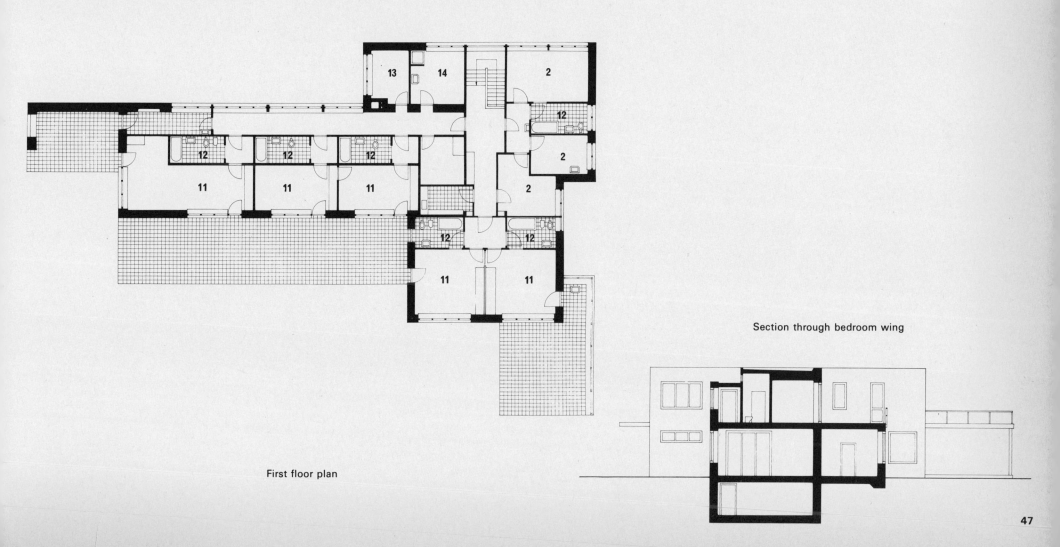

First floor plan

Section through bedroom wing

LOIS WELZENBACHER : Schulz House

1928

Welzenbacher (b.1889) designed many houses in the 1920s which have an easy and undogmatic flow between inside and outside. This house in Westphalia is on a steeply sloping site and has two storeys to the north, with the upper floor living rooms on the same level as the south-facing gardens. The whole window to the living room is lowered electrically into a slot in the floor.

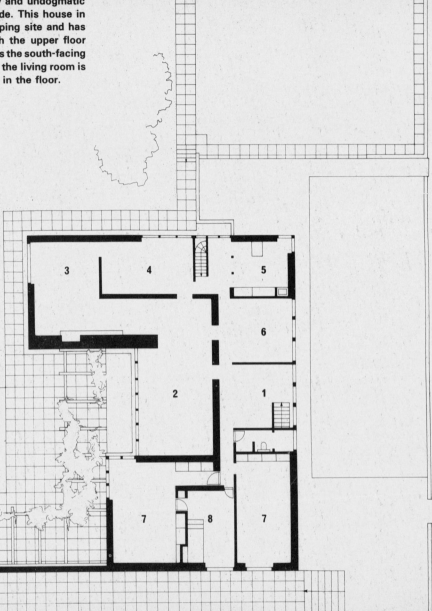

Upper level plan

1 Hall
2 Living room
3 Day room
4 Study
5 Kitchen
6 Dining room
7 Bedroom
8 Bathroom

Construction is brickwork; where it is not structural, as above the living room window, it is laid with joints running vertically. The thick fireplace wall in brick has deeply recessed joints internally. The main rooms of the house are grouped around the garden and the service rooms (which are connected to the main rooms by a separate staircase) are down below.

An enormous bathroom adjoins the parents' bedroom to the east of the living room, indicating its possible use as a gymnasium.

Garden side

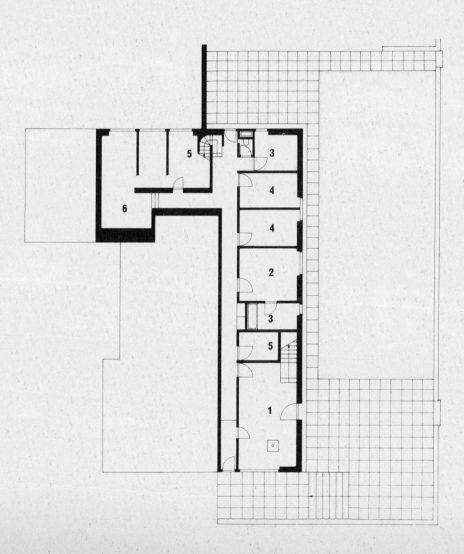

Living room

Lower level plan

1 Entrance
2 Guestroom
3 Bathroom
4 Servant
5 Store
6 Boiler

49

PETER BEHRENS: Berlin-Schlachtensee

1929

Behrens (1868-1940) was in his 60s when he built this house. Its similarity to Gropius's own house (1926) at the Bauhaus is extraordinary. Concrete poured in situ was the material, but while Gropius exploited the possibilities of the cantilevered corner and the porch overhanging both the main and the service entries, Behrens assembled the masses by accentuating in an asymmetrical balance.

The three windows of the upstairs bathroom and the small protruding semicircular bay window, and the layout of doors in the rooms, all suggest these symmetries.

There is a separate flat over the garages. No plans of the basement floor are available.

The house plan simplifies a conventional family life, cladding it in modern garb.

Both this and Behrens' house in the Taunus Mountains were held in high esteem both by P Morton Shand, the amateur guru of the modern movement in Great Britain, and by Raymond McGrath.

Drawn by Richard Porchmouth

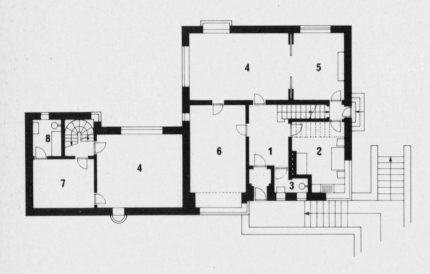

First floor plan

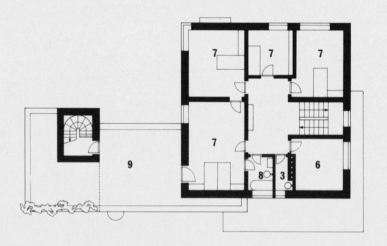

Second floor plan

1 Entrance
2 Kitchen
3 WC
4 Living room
5 Dining room
6 Study
7 Bedroom
8 Bathroom
9 Roof terrace

Entrance front

ERICH MENDELSOHN: Own House
1929

When Mendelsohn (1887-1953) built his own house he eschewed the formalist expressionism of his work in the early twenties and built in the tradition of well-made but unostentatious bourgeois Berlin houses. Luxurious materials were simply but well detailed with occasional modern touches. The living room window, for example, could be lowered electrically, as could the living room windows at Mies' Tugendhat house.

The plan in other terms is fairly conventional; the wide living room extends across the width of the plan and forms the filling between the service rooms below and the bedroom floor above.

Mendelsohn occupied the house for only a short time, leaving in 1933 for England where he stayed till 1941. After that he practised in California.

The work of this migratory period is altogether calmer than that of his expressionistic period, and his own house begins this more mature phase. The house still stands in W. Berlin in the avenue Am Rupenhorn, near the houses by the Luckhardt Brothers (q.v.).

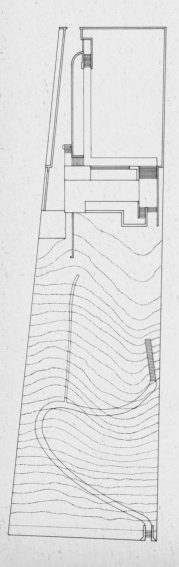

Drawn by David Jennings

Site plan

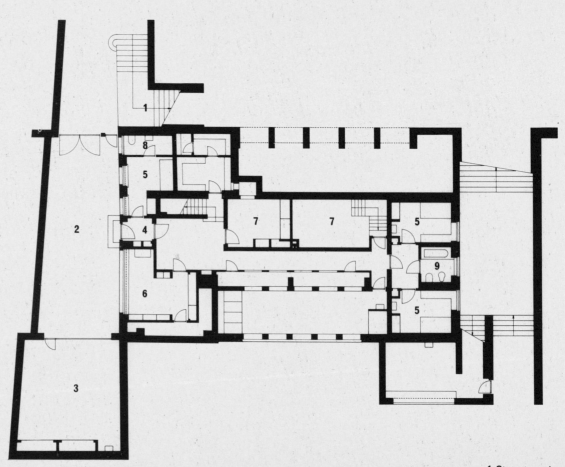

Ground floor plan

1 Steps to main entrance
2 Service court
3 Garage
4 Service entrance
5 Servants
6 Kitchen
7 Store
8 WC
9 Bathroom

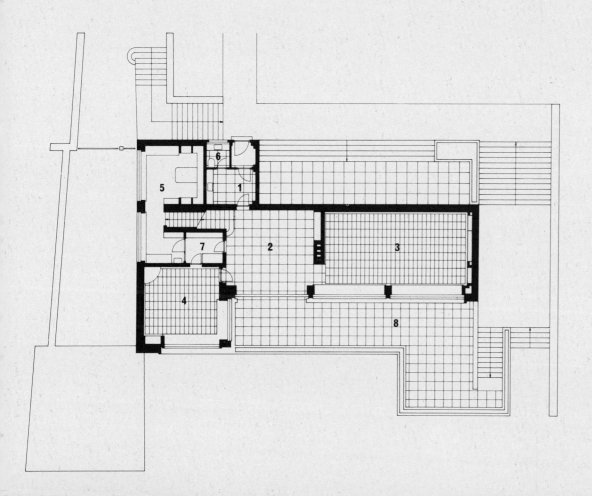

First floor plan

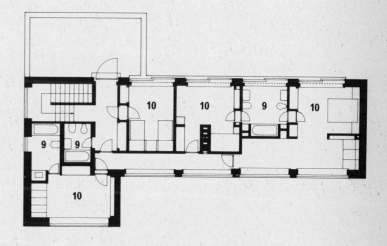

Second floor plan

LE CORBUSIER : Villa Savoie
1930

Now a national monument, this house has become a museum piece because of the celebration Le Corbusier and historians lavished on it. This makes it extremely hard to see it as a house any more, even though it was ever only briefly a weekend retreat. The Corbusian programme of the 20s, the five points, the desire for a transparent but passionate rationale, the celebration of circu-lation in the architectural promenade of the ramp or staircase, and finally the manifest description of architecture made out of forms in light are all united in one building, which almost raises it above analysis.

The problems of its use and furnishing are similar to those of the Villa Stein (qv); but the ingenuity here of the bathroom in the master bedroom opens more possibilities for design. The idea of services as equipment receives a great boost.

Formally the ramp throws the grid of structure given on the outside into a pragmatic muddle so that Le Corbusier can use the column internally for metaphoric more than truly structural effect. On the roof the efflorescence of curved forms

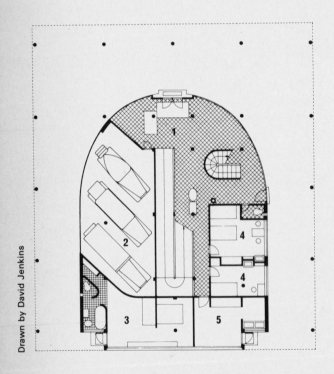

Drawn by David Jenkins

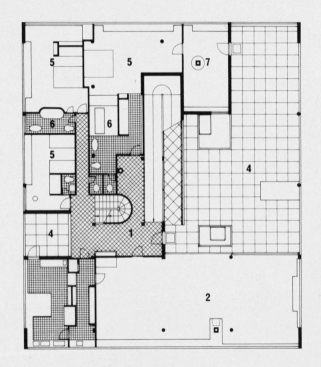

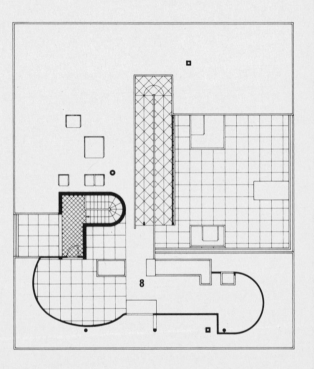

Ground floor plan

1 Entrance
2 Garage
3 Chauffeur's flat
4 Maid's room
5 Laundry

First floor and roof plans

1 Hall
2 Living room
3 Kitchen
4 Terrace
5 Bedroom
6 Bathroom
7 Dressing room
8 Solarium and roof terrace

Entrance elevation

gives an almost surrealistic effect, one that may have derived from Le Corbusier's connections with the patron of Surrealism, Charles de Bestegui, for whom he had just completed a penthouse on the Champs Elysées.

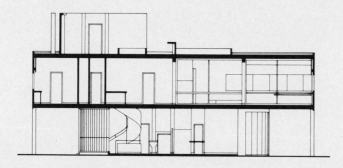

Section through living room

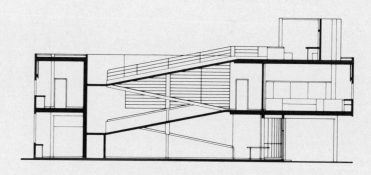

Section through ramp

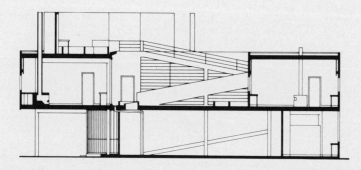

Secton through roof terraces

ADOLF LOOS: Müller House

1930

Loos (1870-1933) wrote about the house in 1930: 'I design no plans, facades, sections, I am designing space. In fact there is neither a ground floor, nor a first floor nor a basement in my designs, there are only integrated rooms, ante-rooms and terraces. Every room requires a specific height – the dining room needs a different one from that of the larder – therefore the ceilings are arranged at different levels. Then one has to integrate all these rooms in such a manner that the transition is not only imperceptible and natural but also functional.' Loos's words have always been more important to writers of architectural history than his buildings. While his text suggests that drawings were not important to him, certainly not as important as the internal spatial complexities, it does imply a completely different tactic from zoning the house horizontally or vertically.

The route occupies the central core. Yet Loos, to whom reticent good taste was the only possibility in buildings, did not make the route such a central event that the spaces of the house appear as adjuncts to its rhetoric – unlike Le Corbusier's

Drawn by Richard Porchmouth

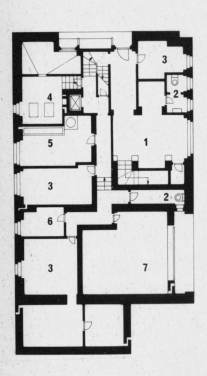
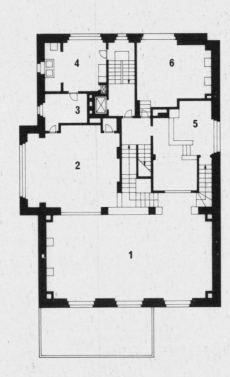
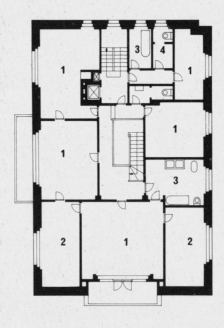
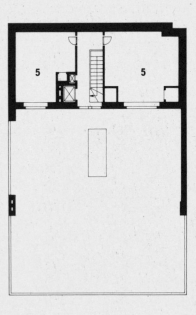

Ground floor plan

1 Entrance
2 WC
3 Store
4 Boiler
5 Kitchen
6 Servant
7 Garage

First floor plan

1 Living room
2 Dining room
3 Servery
4 Kitchen
5 Fr. Muller's room
6 Library

Second and third floor plans

1 Bedroom
2 Dressing room
3 Bathroom
4 WC
5 Servant

Villa Savoie. Each room is finished in accordance with its function, so that in looking through the staircase, the effect is not of looking into a slice of infinite space, but of viewing another space, finished and handled differently.

With notable exceptions, Loos's conception of 'Raumplannung' – spatial planning – has not been developed beyond the level of his works.

The house is to be distinguished from the Möller in Vienna of 1928 and is located in the suburbs of Prague.

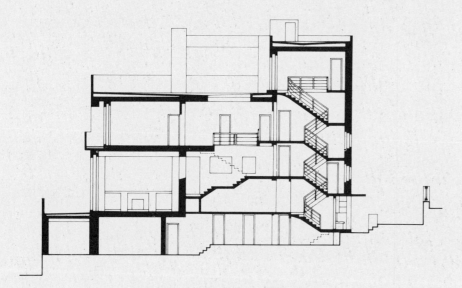

Section

Staircase

MIES VAN DER ROHE: Tugendhat House

1930

From the road the house appears to be single storey. At this level are the sleeping accommodation and entrance hall. From the curved-in entrance, a staircase descends to the lower main living floor. On the east side stretches a conservatory. The main space is divided by a curved partition of dark veneered wood around the dining space and a wall of onyx between the study and the sitting room. The continuous glazing slides down into a pocket in the retaining wall below.

The structure is a grid 5 x 4.6 metres of steel columns sheathed in a cruciform profile of chromium steel. Heating to the main room was ducted hot air; other rooms were heated by radiators. No expense was spared in this house, for which over 300 working drawings were prepared, now all in the Mies van der Rohe Archive at the Museum of Modern Art in New York.

The sense of luxury in the house came not only from the cost of the finishes and the exquisite craftsmanship Mies (1886-1969) demanded, but also from his ability to make a sense of space itself a luxury. In the living rooms, specially designed furniture sits with enough volume around

Drawn by Graham Jahn

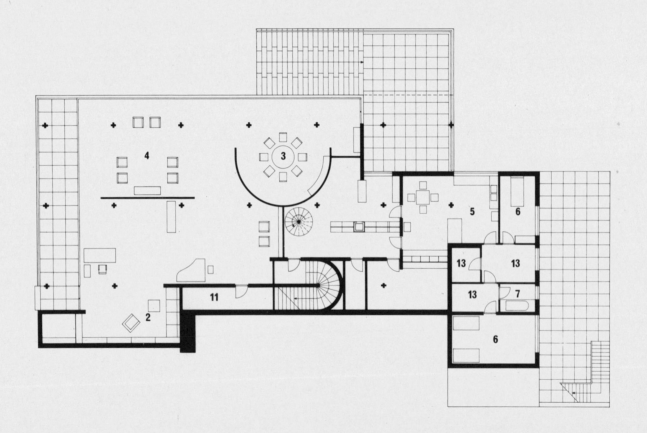

Ground floor plan

1 Entrance	9 Garage
2 Study	10 Chauffeur
3 Dining space	11 WC
4 Sitting space	12 Terrace
5 Kitchen	13 Store
6 Servants	
7 Bathroom	
8 Bedroom	

for each piece to be both isolated and part of a composition inevitably arrived at. If other houses of this period focused on the abandonment of Victorian decorative taste, or on the programme of the new architecture or on some hypothetical union of economics and building, Mies made clear the lesson which the modern movement carried: that tidiness was the name of the game.

The house, in Brno, Czechoslovakia has recently been restored.

Sketch

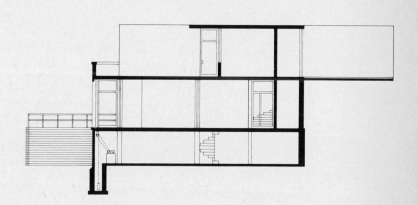

Second floor plan

PIERRE CHAREAU (& BERNARD BIJVOET): Maison de Verre

1931

Chareau (1883-1950) worked with Bijvoet on this Paris house for M. Dalsace. The site, a courtyard off the Rue St Guillaume, had the difficulty of an apartment on the third floor, which had to be retained. Chareau gutted the three floors below and inserted a steel skeleton to support the third-floor flat. Within this frame he put a two-storey house with a double-height living room and a doctor's consulting suite on the ground floor. The spatial diagram of the house is hardly exceptional, but at every point Chareau used modern materials in a most inventive way. Cupboards, bathrooms, wcs, and various kinds of glass walls are all treated as independent pieces of machinery. Chareau's own art deco furniture appears as curiously earthbound by comparison.

A measured survey was published in Yale 'Perspecta' 12, which documents most of the components. The house is now in the hands of a trust, and has been kept in immaculate condition by the family.

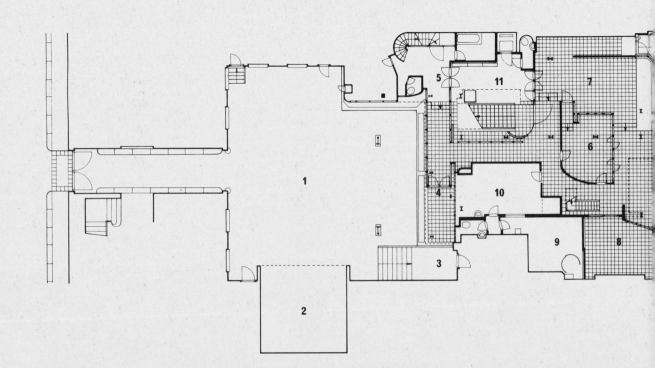

Garden front

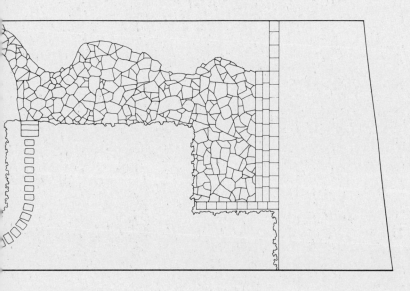

Ground floor plan

1 Forecourt
2 Garage
3 Entrance to existing
apartment
4 Entrance to house and
surgery
5 Service entrance
6 Reception
7 Waiting room
8 Consulting room
9 Examination room
10 Recovery room
11 Entrance hall to
Chareau apartment

Maison de Verre

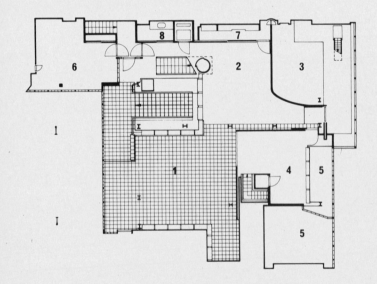

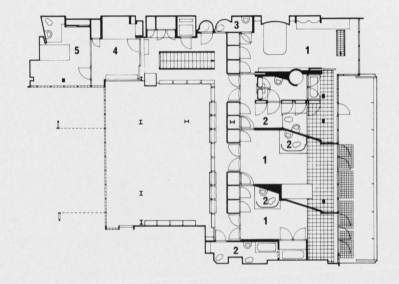

First floor plan

1 Living room
2 Dining room
3 Day room
4 Study
5 Void
6 Kitchen
7 Storage
8 Scullery

Second floor plan

1 Bedroom
2 Bathroom
3 WC
4 Workroom
5 Maid's room
6 Void over living room

Living room

AMYAS CONNELL: New Farm
1932

Built by Amyas Connell (1900-1980) at Haslemere, Surrey for Sir Arthur Lowes-Dickenson, this house reworks the tripartite plan of 'High and Over' completed in 1929, and maintains the planning idea of individual rooms. A staff apartment is tucked away to the north; the owner's rooms all face south. The structure is monolithic concrete 4 inch thick walls, with columns ostentatiously placed in each room. The facade is supported by cantilevers off the frame, allowing windows to continuously wrap around. The flue from the central heating boiler is the structural column supporting the staircase.

A constructivist influence is detected in the plan, but is perhaps more evident in the entry canopy and fireplace in the living room, both of which have strong surrealistic overtones.

Ground floor plan

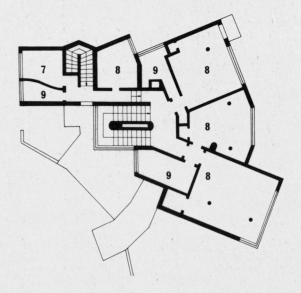

First floor plan

Drawn by Lucia Mortato

1 Entrance
2 Sitting room
3 Study
4 Dining room
5 Kitchen
6 Store
7 Servant
8 Bedroom
9 Bathroom

Garden front

HUGO HÄRING: Courtyard House Project

1932

This project was for a proposed exhibition of houses in Stuttgart to be completed five years after the Weissenhof Siedlung. The rise to power of the Nazis stopped it. Häring (1882-1958), with Scharoun, was the most famous of the younger expressionist architects; his fame rests upon the farm buildings at Gut Garkau, where each function was given a distinctive form. There the construction provided the binding element; and in this project construction dominates the design ideas. The courtyards are relaxed spaces within a totally private world. They could easily be compared with the contemporary courtyard projects of Mies van der Rohe, in which Mies ordered the plan as a play between a perimeter and the minimum of enclosing walls. Häring took a less doctrinaire approach, and produced something less memorable but something nonetheless which prefigured much post-war planning. Architecture with a human face was already here promoted as dependent on small-scale construction, that brand of functionalist theory which did not wish to invent forms.

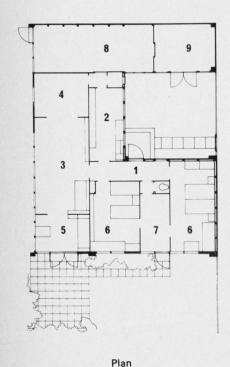

Drawn by Paul Gregory

Plan

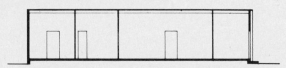

Section through courtyard showing entrance

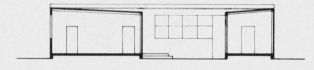

Long section through living room

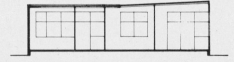

Section through bedrooms

Long section through courtyard

1 Entrance
2 Kitchen
3 Living
4 Dining
5 Study
6 Bedroom
7 Bath
8 Garage
9 Store

Axonometric

JOSÉ LUIS SERT: Galobart House

1932

Sert (1902-1983) built this house adjacent to an existing one. His scheme wraps around the garden side and links his new living rooms to the garden by ramp. The architect's expressed intention was to give these rooms the greatest spatial feeling in relation to the existing garden. A service stair to one side connects the maid's rooms, kitchen, and stores; the main bedrooms are conventionally enough on the floor above the living rooms, and most open onto a terrace, which is treated as the terrace to the entrance front of Le Corbusier's Villa Stein.

The house has an inside reinforced concrete wall and frame structure, which Sert used as the garden facade, to suggest that the house stood on pilotis.

The house was suppressed from his 'collected works' volume of 1967.

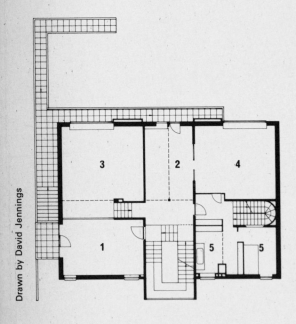

Drawn by David Jennings

First floor plan

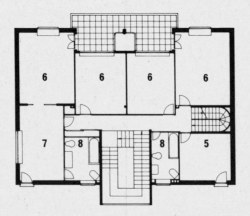

Second floor plan

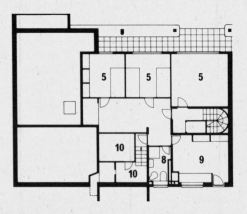

Basement

1 Entrance
2 Hall
3 Living room
4 Study
5 Servant
6 Bedroom
7 Dressing room
8 Bathroom
9 Kitchen
10 Store

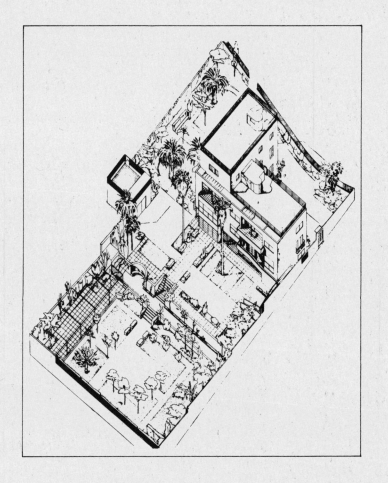

Axonometric

HANS SCHAROUN: Schmunke House

1933

This steel frame, long, thin house sails out across its landscape with every nautical metaphor blaring. The literal transparency of the living room, which runs like a spine through the plan, allows Scharoun (1893-1972) to reduce any conventional idea of circulation to a minimum. Where staircases connect the two floors of protruding terraces, they are employed almost as sun breakers to the completely glazed end of the living space.

In the plan an illusion of openness contrasts with the series of incidents, which reaches a crescendo at the overlapping terraces. This excitement contrasts with the 'base' of purely functional rooms (bedrooms, service spaces) which acts as a cornice and produces a surface which extends and wraps around the terraces. More than many other houses, this takes part in the passage of the seasons, while teetering on the edge of total incoherence. In any last analysis, the discipline of the plan saves the house from being just too many visual tricks.

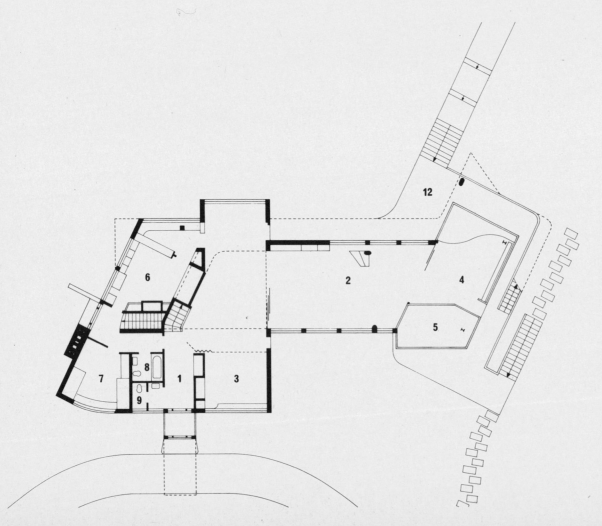

Ground floor plan

Drawn by Geraldine Walder

Living room

Conservatory

1 Hall
2 Living room
3 Play room
4 Dining room
5 Conservatory
6 Kitchen
7 Store

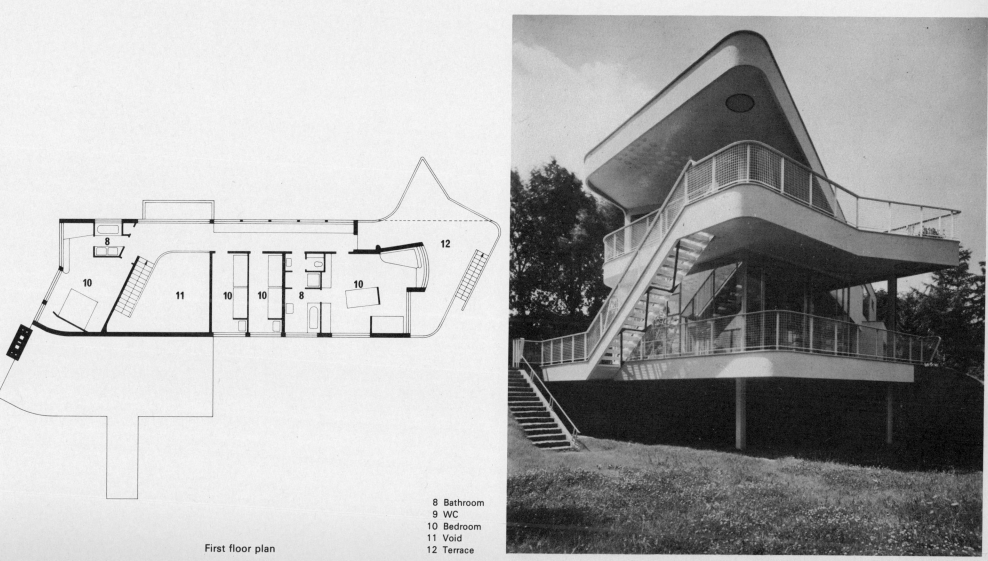

Living room terraces

First floor plan

8 Bathroom
9 WC
10 Bedroom
11 Void
12 Terrace

71

WILLIAM LESCAZE: Own House

1934

Lescaze (1896-1969) built this town house for himself. Its whiteness, protrusion into the street, and glaring indifference to 19th-century New York can leave some commentators cold.

The plan is much deeper than is common in Europe, and adopts an almost Amsterdam-like section: Lescaze kept his drawing office in the lower ground, entered to the right of the facade,

while his quarters are reached by entering up the stairs to the left, under a cantilevered canopy. A further straight flight arrives at the bedroom floor and then returns over itself to the top floor living room, which extends from front to back a distance of nearly 50 feet (over 15 metres).

All glazing to the front, except windows to the kitchen and maid's room, is glass block – the first

use of this material in America. The house is completely air conditioned.

The suspicion from the plan is that Lescaze saw his own house as a private place, because in order for visitors to go from dining room to living room they had to rise two storeys through the bedroom floor. The inconvenience of this may derive from the narrowness of the site.

Ground floor plan

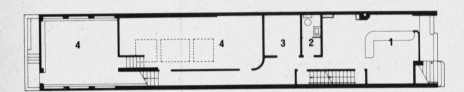

Second floor plan

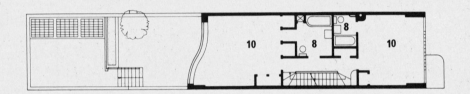

First floor plan

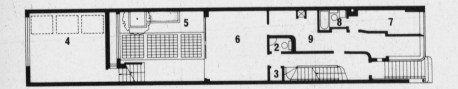

Third floor plan

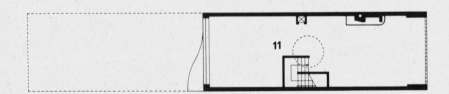

Drawn by Mike Emptage

1 Office reception
2 WC
3 Store
4 Draughting room
5 Terrace
6 Study
7 Servants
8 Bathroom
9 Kitchen
10 Bedroom
11 Living room

Street elevation

KOCHER & FREY: Aluminaire House

1931

Metal construction – aluminium in the first case, steel in the second – formed the basis for these two houses on pilotis designed by Kocher (1885-1969) and Frey (1903-), exhibited at the Architectural and Allied Arts Exposition, New York, 1931, then recreated at Syosset, Long Island by Wallace Harrison. The 3 inch (75mm) thick walls of the first house are possibly the thinnest achieved.

The second house was a mixed construction of steel frame with wooden frame infill. External blinds shielded the glazing, and the plan is of an 'existenz minimum' close to intolerable outside the demands of a holiday home.

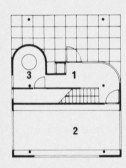

Ground floor plan

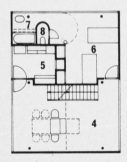

First floor plan

Second floor plan

1 Entrance
2 Garage
3 Plant
4 Living
5 Kitchen
6 Bedroom
7 Bathroom
8 WC
9 Terrace

Elevation

Undercroft

First floor plan

1 Kitchen
2 Dining
3 Living
4 Sleeping
5 Bathroom

Front elevation

WELLS COATES: Studio
1935

Coates (1895-1958) built this apartment for himself on an upper floor, only 12 feet high, of a mews house in Knightsbridge. The sectional planning occurred where he installed the kitchen and bathroom, above which he contrived two separate sleeping spaces by using the height over cupboards as walkways. The one window is fully double-glazed, with a garden trough between the two panes. Air from the mews is drawn in and filtered. Heating is from the ceiling and an electric fire. The colour scheme was white, with ivory, copper, and Eton blue for the fittings. All furniture was specially designed. The purpose-made window frames were made up from stock steel sections.

This small but efficiently planned apartment, with its sitting on the floor 'la japonais', is a model of ingenuity and invention.

Coates installed a radio 'exposed to view as planned by the engineer. . . There is something uncanny about the "scale" of modern equipment of this kind: at certain angles of view you could imagine this set as a huge power station.' The pleasure of architecture was indeed doing more

Drawn by Heidi Löcker

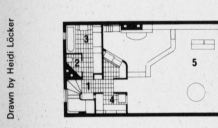

Plan

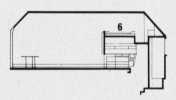

Section through kitchen

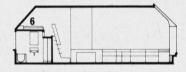

Section through bathroom

1 Entrance
2 WC
3 Bathroom
4 Kitchen
5 Living
6 Bedspace

with less, and then imagining more in what had
been lessened.

Living room

FIGINI & POLLINI: House in Milan

1935

Built as part of the Milan Triennale in the Villagio dei Giornalisti, this house subsequently became Figini's own house. The partners (both born in 1903) contributed to the growth of Italian Rationalism, and together with Terragni sought a pure and tectonic architecture. It is surprising therefore to find this house conforming so easily to Le Corbusier's five principles, and indeed being

more pure than his own Villa Savoie, and more reasonable in that the first floor is lifted so high off the ground that the Italian sun has little trouble striking the earth underneath the house.

The tree inside the two-storey high patio at one end also recalls that celebrated image of Le Corbusier's Pavillon de l'Esprit Nouveau.

The house, now surrounded by vegetation, has

survived remarkably well; but — with the house by Terragni — it is evidence that the rationalists of this epoch never became as interested in house design as in the design of public works.

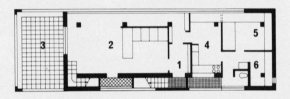

First floor plan

Second floor plan

Section

Drawn by Geraldine Walder

1 Entrance	6 Store
2 Living room	7 WC
3 Terrace	8 Bathroom
4 Kitchen	9 Bedroom
5 Servant	10 Void

Elevation

Living room terrace

FRANK LLOYD WRIGHT: Falling Water

1935

This guest house in Bear Run, Pennsylvania, for the Kaufmann family was designed after a fallow period for Wright but in the same year as the Johnson Wax Administration Building. The idea for cantilevered terraces is said to have come to Wright (1867-1959) in an instant.

Wright's materials are those of international modernism: white balconies, but thicker than in Germany or France because of their structural duties; horizontally banded glazing throughout and the dramatic gravity-defying cantilevers. The influence of De Stijl is very much in evidence though Wright takes only that which has a place in his American romance: the desire to give form to the American dream. Wright began to design the Usonian houses in the same year as designing Falling Water.

A paradox of this house is that it has come to represent modern architecture to countless architects, though the trek to the building makes it more celebrated in photos than in reality. Yet it has never been imitated. The power of its image is stronger than its power as an archetype.

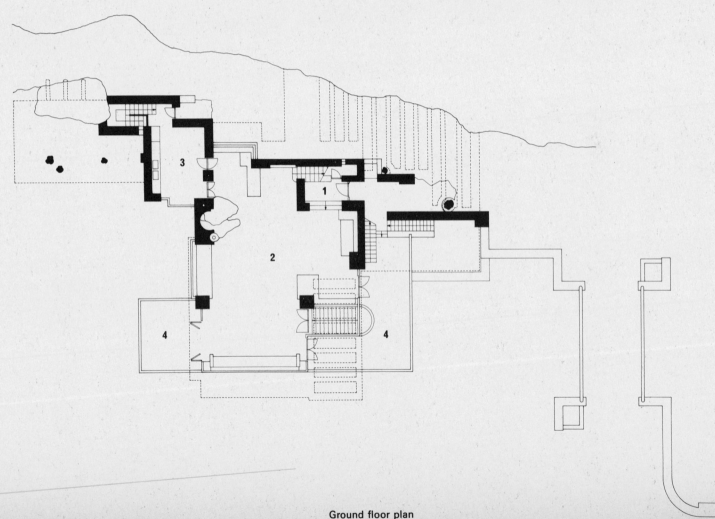

Drawn by David Jennings

Ground floor plan

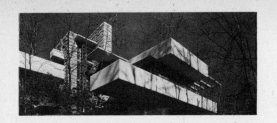

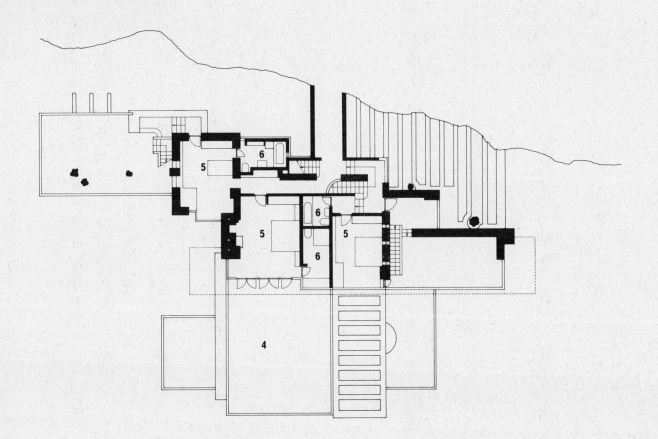

First floor plan

1 Entrance
2 Living room
3 Kitchen
4 Terrace
5 Bedroom
6 Bathroom

Falling Water

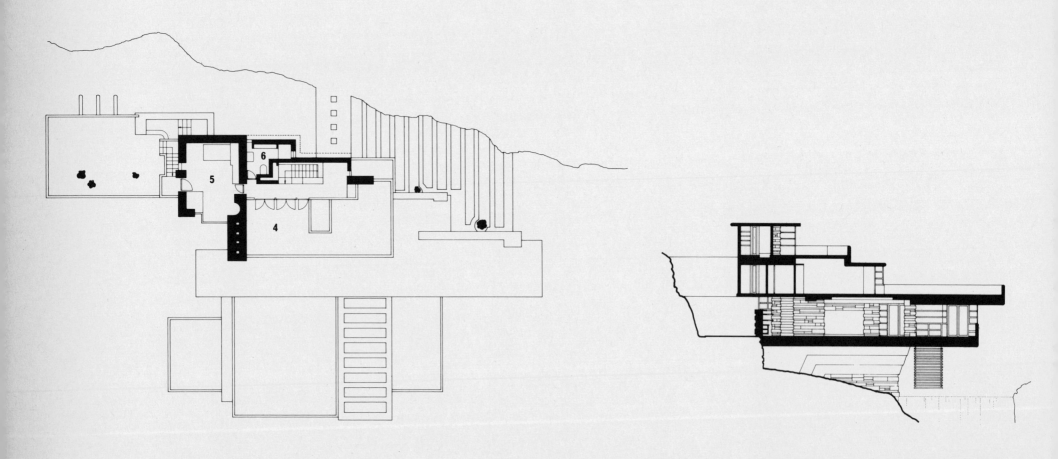

Second floor plan

Section

FRANK LLOYD WRIGHT: Usonian House

1935

One of the earliest of the many Usonian houses built by Wright to provide a generic solution to the problem of designing a small house at moderate cost, the Jacobs House wraps around an acre of garden, with its entrance in the corner. Wright listed nine points that this house avoided: no visible roofs, garage, basement, 'trim' inside, radiators or light fittings, not much furniture or bric-a-brac, no painting of surfaces, no plaster nor gutters. Five materials only were used: wood, brick, cement, paper, and glass.

Bathroom and kitchen were adjacent, to economize on service runs; but Wright did include a cellar for the heating plant that provided ducted warm air. Bedrooms and study are interchangeable: both are workrooms or sleeping rooms. Each room facing the garden also opens to it.

If there is a criticism, it is the large amount of corridor needed to reach the bedrooms and study.

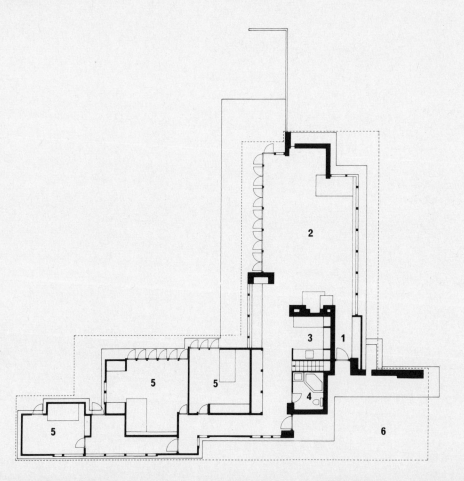

1 Entrance
2 Living room
3 Kitchen
4 Bathroom
5 Bedroom
6 Carport

Drawn by David Jennings

BERTHOLD LUBETKIN: House at Whipsnade

1936

Two similar houses were built on the Whipsnade Zoo's estate; this, the first was for Lubetkin (1901-) and his family. Neither agreeing with the earthbound romanticism of Frank Lloyd Wright nor wishing to have the landscape flow into the house and vice-versa, this building – like the communal spaces of Le Corbusier's Pavillon Suisse – floats on the site. Its concrete frame has modular windows. The frame is juxtaposed with a curved screen wall oriented for sun and to highlight the entrance. Inside, a diminutive variant of the curved screen repeats the device here associated with the dining room by Le Corbusier in the Villa Stein and Mies van der Rohe in the Tugendhat House. Coe and Reading in 'Lubetkin and Tecton, Architecture and Social Commitment'

associate it with Soane's breakfast parlour in his own house.

The plan could not be more simply zoned, with one function occupying each of the three arms. In all Lubetkin's work the logic of its design and how it is constructed mesh together without any mystery, but with great care.

Drawn by Simon Colebrook

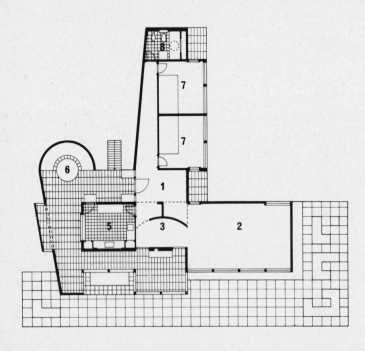

Ground floor plan

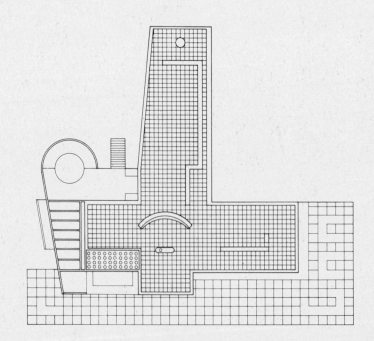

Roof plan

1 Entrance
2 Living room
3 Dining
4 Loggia
5 Kitchen
6 Solarium
7 Bedroom
8 Bathroom

84

Aerial view

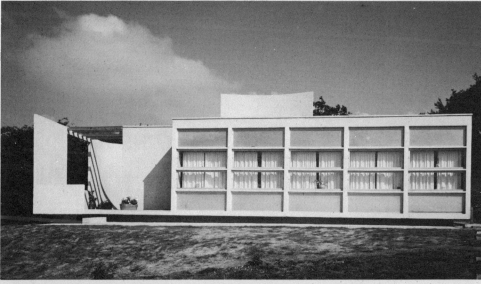

Front elevation

Interior

GIUSEPPE TERRAGNI : Villa Bianca
1937

Terragni (1904-1943) built only two private houses, though two more were projected. This one for his engineer cousin is volumetrically similar to the other house outside Como. But here the long rectangular solid is entered in the centre, with living rooms to one side and services to the other. Bedrooms occupy the first floor, through which a staircase leads externally to a roof terrace.

In the living rooms a protrusion to the front houses a study, which appears on the elevation as a box within a box. The windows too are in frames which extend beyond the wall plane of the house. The flat cantilevered slabs at roof level are more of a mystery, hinting at an incomplete overhanging cornice, or simply as themselves planes which cast a dramatic shadow over an otherwise un-modulated plane.

The villa is now a restaurant and is well-looked after by its owners. It is located in Seveso near Milan.

Basement plan

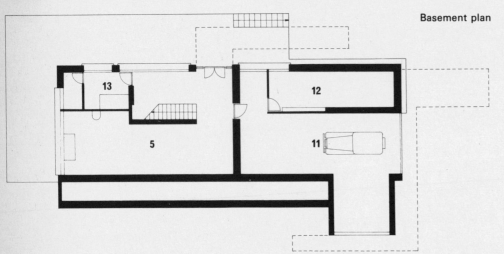

First floor plan

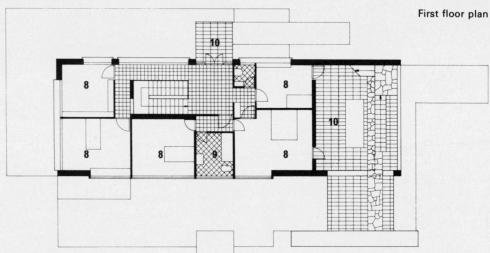

Ground floor plan

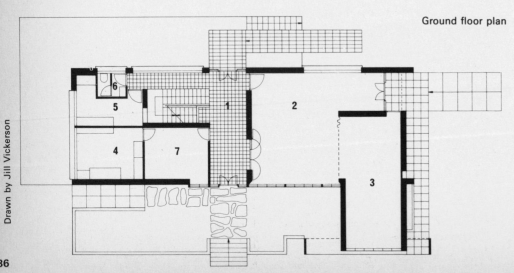

Roof plan

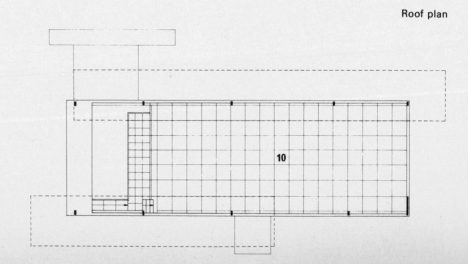

Drawn by Jill Vickerson

1 Entrance   8 Bedroom
2 Living room   9 Bathroom
3 Study   10 Terrace
4 Kitchen   11 Garage
5 Utility   12 Store
6 WC   13 Servant
7 Breakfast room

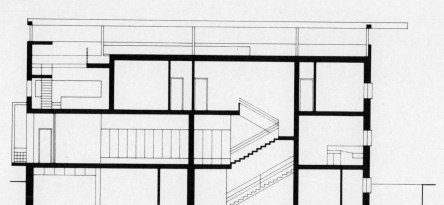

Long section through staircase

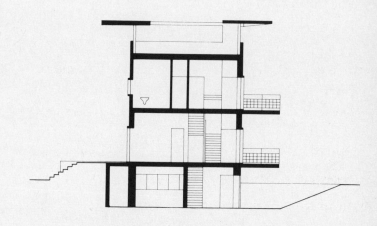

Cross section through entrance

Long section through kitchen and living room

Cross section through study

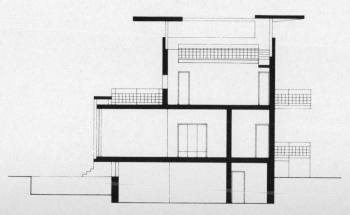

SERGE CHERMAYEFF: Bentley Wood

1938

The story of how the modern movement came to England is well rehearsed. Chermayeff (born 1900) designed this house as a two-storey frame attached at right angles to a long single-storey high wall containing garage and servant spaces, pierced by the entrance into the back court of the house. The two-storey part of the house is zoned into a narrow band to the north, consisting of service rooms on both floors. To the south the glazed plane of the facade connects all living spaces, and above each bedroom enjoins an exterior partly covered terrace.

Construction is brick load-bearing walls covered by cedar boarding. All large windows were in teak frames sliding on bronze tracks.

From the south the house acts as a wall to harbour the lawn. The vertical grid terminating the long single-storey wall is a miniature version of the grid of columns on the facade of the house, and the proportions repeat those of mullions and transoms in the large living room windows.

This economy somehow is at odds with a very large and lavish country house, more a re-working of that idea in modern movement terms than a

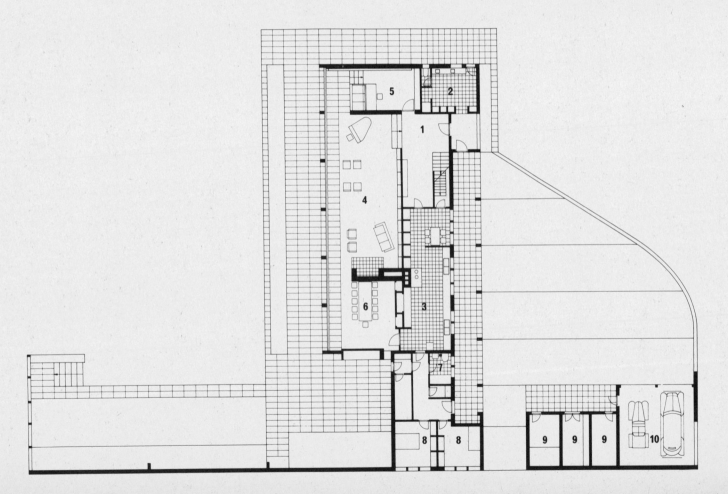

Ground floor plan

house which promotes a more egalitarian way of life. Chermayeff's later work went further in that direction in advocating the patio house as one which gave children spaces more independent of their parents' spaces than this house seems to, even if all bedrooms are isolated from corridors by a double bank of cupboards and the parents and children are at opposite ends of the upper floor.

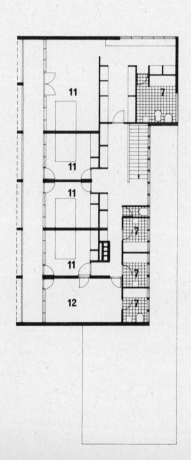

1 Entrance
2 Utility
3 Kitchen
4 Living room
5 Study
6 Dining
7 Bathroom
8 Servant
9 Stores
10 Garage
11 Bedroom
12 Childrens' room

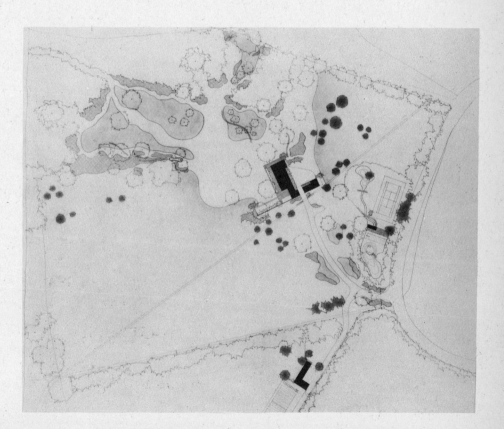

First floor plan

Site plan

Bentley Wood

1 Site view
2 Entrance front

3 Garden front
4 Living room
5 Looking to screen

Terrace

CONNELL WARD & LUCAS: 66 Frognal

1938

The architects Connell, Ward (1902-1918), Lucas (1906-1984) faced the same local opposition to this scheme as they had overcome earlier in the 30s, for houses at Rickmansworth. A small corner site meant placing the house close to the road to maximize the garden, to which the entire house opens up in a vast glazed and terraced facade. The owners specifically required that rooms should be lit from one side only.

The first floor is effectively the owners' flat. The children's rooms are on the second floor and their playroom is at ground level, so these two parts can be closed while the children were away at boarding school. All furniture, except chairs, tables, and beds, was purpose-made to be built-in.

The section is universally applicable to the house as a type; individualistic details have a high degree of finish. With this house, modern architecture in England came of age—and showed how constructionally and aesthetically the ideals of the Modern Movement could be adapted to the British climate.

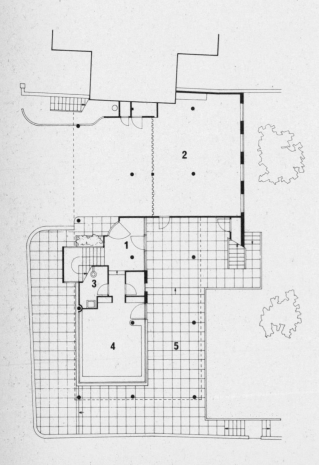

Drawn by Mike Russum

Ground floor plan

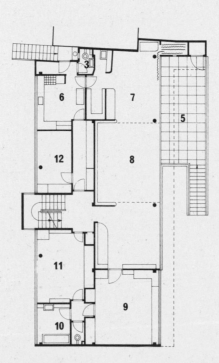

First floor plan

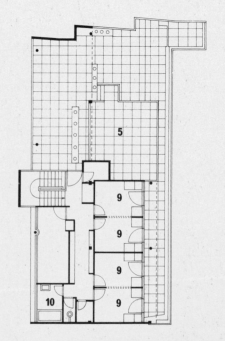

Second floor plan

1 Entrance	7 Dining room
2 Garage	8 Living room
3 WC	9 Bedroom
4 Childrens' room	10 Bathroom
5 Terrace	11 Study
6 Kitchen	12 Guestroom

Section

Living room

Street elevation

Garden side

93

ERNÖ GOLDFINGER: Willow Road

1939

Goldfinger (born 1902) came to London in 1934 from Le Corbusier's office in Paris. He built his own house five years later, the central house of a group of three on a sloping site near Hampstead Heath. Like Lubetkin, a committed modernist, he nonetheless believed in using local materials, and so brick – not plaster or concrete – is the facing for the building, which is supported by a reinforced concrete frame.

The house is unified externally by a long window which crosses the party wall and is surrounded by a protruding concrete frame. The living rooms are all on the floor above the entrance – two storeys above the garden, such is the slope of the site. The two end houses have living rooms facing east with balconies; Goldfinger's house in the middle section faces west. A demand for privacy between the houses is thereby respected.

Ground floor plan

Basement plan

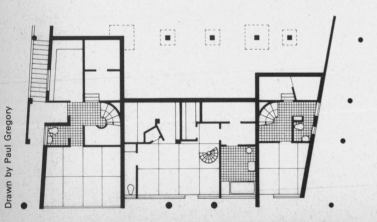

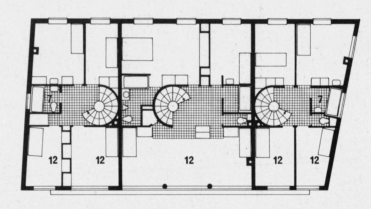

First floor plan

Second floor plan

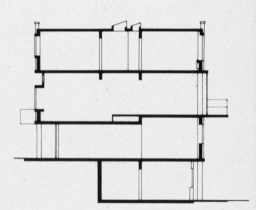

Section

1 Entrance	7 Bathroom
2 Garage	8 Store
3 Laundry	9 Living room
4 Maid's room	10 Kitchen
5 Guestroom	11 Studio
6 Garden room	12 Bedroom

Drawn by Paul Gregory

Living room

Garden front

Dining room

Front elevation

95

DENYS LASDUN: Newton Road
1939

Completed by Lasdun (b.1914) when he was only 25, this clean and elegant town house nods in Le Corbusier's direction. The house, built between working for Wells Coates and Tecton, has a strict symmetry externally which relaxes slightly inside. At ground floor level are the servants' quarters and a garage. At first floor level an L-shaped dining/living room wraps around the staircase, leaving a corner for a study. Bedrooms occupy the second floor, where the staircase effectively ends. From this floor access to the studio floor is on one corner, allowing maximum floor area for this, the largest space in the house.

Ground floor plan

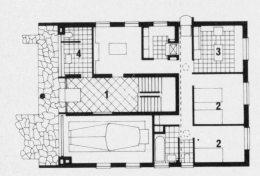

First floor plan

Second floor plan

Third floor plan

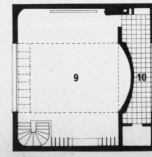

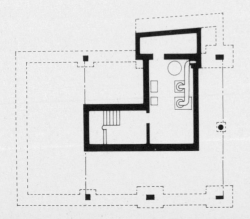

Basement plan

Front to back section

Drawn by Heidi Löcker

1 Entrance	6 Living and dining room
2 Servant	7 Study
3 Kitchen	8 Bedroom
4 WC	9 Studio
5 Bathroom	10 Terrace

Living room

Staircase

Front elevation

MARCEL BREUER & WALTER GROPIUS: Chamberlain Cottage

1941

Breuer's (1902-1981) understanding of American timber balloon frame constructed on a masonry base is intelligently exaggerated in this house, designed soon after his leaving Europe. The balloon frame is constructed as a truss, allowing cantilevering of the kitchen and 'ingle nook' over the lower ground floor entrance, as well as the glazed porch at right angles to the kitchen.

The plan is divided into a narrow zone for the kitchen, bathroom and dressing room, with the bedroom and living room in the deeper adjacent zone. A fireplace divides the living area into dining and sitting spaces.

In Europe such a house could easily have become a prototype but for the demands it makes on the site, because it has views in all directions.

In America and in Great Britain, the typical qualities of this little cottage were transposed into a formula for a 'relaxed' weekend retreat. In this new formula, for which the original architects cannot be held responsible, the possibility for individual expression slipped in behind the logical and rigorous Bauhaus understanding of the problems of building in the 20th century.

Drawn by Simon Colebrook

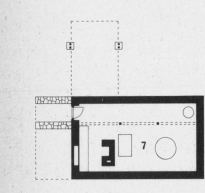

Basement plan

Upper plan

1 Entrance platform
2 Bathroom
3 Kitchen
4 Dressing room
5 Bedroom
6 Living room
7 Store

Side elevation

Entrance elevation

OSCAR NIEMEYER: Own House

1942

Writing in 1950, Niemeyer (1907-) saw architecture in Brazil responding to the inheritance of 'orthodox functionalism' and the baroque architecture of the colonial period. But he was disappointed that his work could not be better because technical and social forces were out of balance. His subsequent close personal friendship with Kubitschek, the president and driving force behind Brasilia, may have ameliorated this problem in his own eyes.

His own house built in 1942 in the Gavea district of Rio de Janeiro is both a homage and a step towards Brazilian architecture. Taking the five points from Le Corbusier, he adjusted the double-height volume into a central space, at the back of which a ramp connects two zones – one for sleeping, the other a studio open to the central living room. Natural stone is used for the only short wall there, and suggests – with the living room, and the monopitched roof – a nascent regionalism.

The house was kept small in site coverage to maximize a small but lush garden. A striped blind protects the terrace which comes almost to the

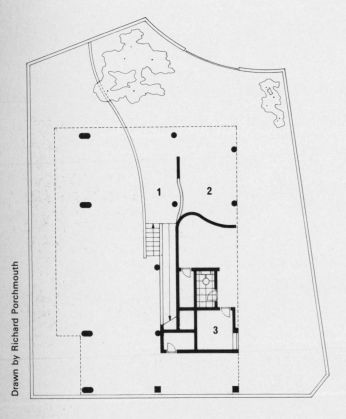

Drawn by Richard Porchmouth

Ground floor plan

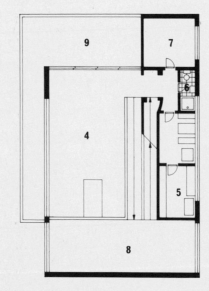

First floor plan

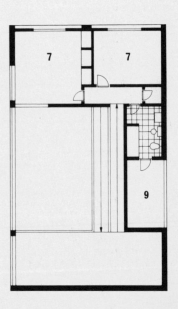

Second floor plan

1 Entrance   6 WC
2 Garage   7 Bedroom
3 Servant   8 Studio
4 Living room   9 Terrace
5 Kitchen

edge of the plot line. Between the 20s and 50s, houses like this began to explore the reconciliations that might be possible between the modern movement and its later developments.

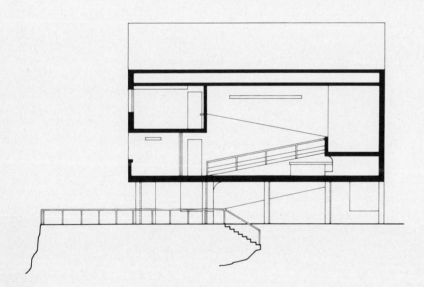

Section

Street elevation

AMANCIO WILLIAMS: Country House
1944

Built at Mar del Plata, this small house achieves a large scale because it is conceived as a bridge. When first published in Europe, Williams' (b.1913) house was compared with Ledoux's House for a Director of the Loue of 1775, an early example of historicism entering the modern tradition. Certainly the stream the house bridges hardly warrants the gesture, but the idea of a bridge/house is consistently and rhetorically worked through.

A curve supports walls in reinforced concrete, on which the single storey sits. The concrete is board-marked and aggregate was very particularly chosen. Internally, two staircases connect to a long narrow living space, the bridge of a ship, with service rooms and bedrooms on the shaded side. The interior of each room is meticulously handled, with exemplary workmanship – all to the credit of the architect and his on-site builders, given the great distance of the site from centres of industry.

The modern movement again shows itself as an unfinished project, which here becomes a matter of formal and technical invention, even nodding towards historical allusion.

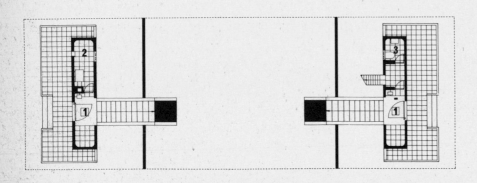

Ground floor plan

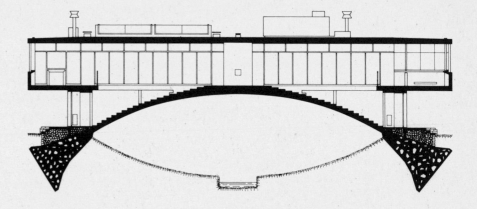

Long section

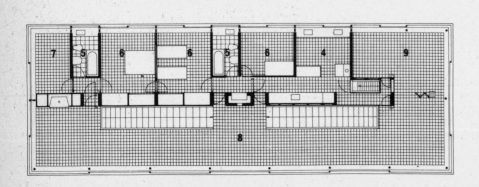

First floor plan

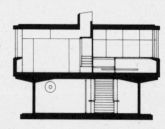

Cross section

1 Entrance
2 Service
3 WC
4 Kitchen
5 Bathroom
6 Bedroom
7 Dressing room
8 Living room
9 Dining room

Drawn by David Jennings